BRISTOL LIVES

To Tim on your 70th
Ann & Andrew
2011

BRISTOL LIVES

MAURICE FELLS

SilverWood
originals

Published in paperback by SilverWood Books 2011
www.silverwoodbooks.co.uk

This book is a SilverWood Original – traditional publishing at its best

ISBN 978-1-906236-42-7

British Library Cataloguing in Publication Data
A CIP catalogue record for this book is available from the British Library

Set in Palatino by SilverWood Books

Printed in England on paper certified as being from sustainable sources

BRISTOL LIVES

Introduction

Since my schooldays I have been fascinated by the bountiful and rich history of my native city. Many a happy childhood hour was spent searching for the background to a newly discovered plaque or statue.

It's a history greatly enhanced by the pioneering spirit manifested by explorers, industrialists, entrepreneurs and benefactors who were either born here or had strong connections with the city. Some names, like that of the explorer John Cabot, the engineer Isambard Kingdom Brunel and the poet Thomas Chatterton, have been woven into the fabric of our heritage. However, other people who helped to shape today's environment are hardly remembered now; for example, Dr William Budd, who earned the sobriquet 'Father of Health' for his pioneering work in preventative medicine and Sir George White, who not only gave Bristol its tram and bus system but also its aircraft industry.

Not all those who walk through the pages of this book are from Bristol's dim and distant past. Dr Beryl Corner, for example, was very much a woman of the twentieth century. She may have been small in stature but did not let her male colleagues with all their prejudices walk over her. With true grit, determination and an iron will she broke down barriers that stopped women advancing their careers in medicine. Along the way she founded Bristol's first special baby care unit. Dr Corner became an inspiration for other women wanting to work in her profession.

In this book you will also meet the priest they called the 'Red Bishop', the businessman who was promised a cabbage a year in return for his help in establishing an inner city farm on land where his home once stood, and the brothers who changed a nation's eating habits. There's also the inventor of a so-called thrashing machine for errant schoolchildren, and the family who gave thousands of people a job for life with their firm, whose brand became a national and international household name.

The aim of my book is to acknowledge the achievements of fellow Bristolians past and present, and give them the recognition they may not have received but truly deserve. These biographies are by no means definitive but they help to paint a picture of Bristol and its great maritime and commercial heritage as it developed from a small port to become one of England's major cities.

Maurice Fells

Acknowledgements

As a passionate Bristolian the research and writing of this book has been a labour of love. Much enjoyable time was spent reading yellowing and torn copies of old newspapers. Early editions of the *Western Daily Press*, founded in the middle of the 19th century, and the *Bristol Evening Post*, which first rolled off the presses in 1932, were rich sources of information.

My own archive of 'house magazines', press releases and other publicity material issued by old established Bristol firms, now swallowed up by multinational conglomerates, has also proved invaluable. Various publications by Redcliffe Press were consulted, and *Chambers Biographical Dictionary* has become a trusted friend, especially for birth, death and other anniversary dates.

Members of the staff at Bristol Central Library and Bristol Records Office were most patient and courteous in dealing with my many enquiries to fill some of the gaps.

I am extremely grateful to Mildred and Francis Ford for granting me access to their extensive archive of old Bristol postcards, some of which add much interest to this book.

Thanks must go also to Helen Hart at SilverWood Books for her faith in accepting my manuscript and turning it into this book.

Finally, I owe a special debt of gratitude and affection to Janet and Trevor Naylor for their undying enthusiasm and encouragement in this project.

Maurice Fells
Bristol

BRISTOL LIVES

Scipio Africanus

(1702—1720)

In the churchyard of St Mary the Virgin at Henbury, about six miles north-west of the city centre, there are many tombstones, that stand at decidedly precarious angles, in want of tender loving care. Their inscriptions have faded down the centuries making it almost impossible for us to read about those lying at rest there.

But thanks to a recent restoration of the tomb of Scipio Africanus we can at least glean a little information about him. Not only is there an elaborately painted headstone, with black cherub faces, but also a footstone.

The headstone simply states that Scipio was a Negro servant to the Rt Honourable Charles William Howard, the seventh Earl of Suffolk and Bindon, and that he died on the 21st December 1720 aged eighteen years.

The footstone is inscribed with a verse which begins:

I, who was born a pagan and a slave,
Now sweetly sleep a Christian in my grave

Little is known about Scipio Africanus save that he came from West Africa and is believed to have been named after a Roman general. He became a servant at the Great House, Henbury, where he was engaged for about five years. This was the home of Charles Howard and his wife Arabella Astry who both died two years after the death of Scipio. The Great House was demolished in 1960.

We shall never know How Scipio Africanus arrived at Henbury and was employed by one of the wealthiest families in Henbury village at the time. We are aware, of course, that Bristol played a prominent role in the slave trade in the 18th century. It was a legal activity at the time but is now viewed with great abhorrence. The tomb of Scipio Afircanus is one of the very few memorials to African slaves.

29A. GORILLA 'ALFRED'.

AT THE BRISTOL ZOO.

PHOTO 'WESTERN DAILY PRESS'.

PURCHASED BY THE BRISTOL ZOO
ON 5/9/30 WHEN HE WAS ABOUT
2 YEARS OLD.

*Alfred the gorilla at home
in Bristol Zoo.*

Alfred
(?—1948)

During the 1930s and 1940s he was one of the most popular residents of Bristol and had a worldwide following.

Non-Bristolians are often surprised and even amused at the fuss that's made to maintain the memory of Alfred who died more than fifty years ago. He was no great soldier, no statesmen, no scientist or explorer — but a gorilla.

After his death a firm of taxidermists mounted his skin which is still on display in Bristol's City Museum and Art Gallery and a bronze cast of his head is on show at Bristol Zoo.

Alfred was bought for £350 in 1930 by the zoo where he lived until his death eighteen years later. An orphan gorilla from the Congo, his parents had been shot whilst raiding farmers' fields for food.

From the day of his arrival in Bristol Alfred was a big hit, not only with his keepers but with the many thousands of visitors to the zoo each year. He often met them while being taken by a keeper for walks around the gardens, always wearing his distinctive woolly jumper.

His continuing weight gains were the talk of the town so a special weighing machine was installed and visitors were invited to guess Alfred's weight. In 1938 he tipped the scales at just over twenty-six stone.

Picture postcards of him were sent all over the world, many of them by American servicemen based in Bristol during the Second World War. Such was his popularity that he even received greetings cards on his official birthday — September 5th, the day he arrived at the zoo.

When he died zoo officials announced that his death was caused by a low-flying aircraft that made him panic and collapse. However, unknown to his numerous admirers Alfred had been suffering from tuberculosis for a year. Such was his fame that his death was reported throughout the country.

Richard Amerike

(1445 —1503)

What's in a name? Quite a lot it seems, if it happens to be Richard ap Meryk or Amerike who is said to have lent his name to the most powerful nation in the world. Some historians, however, argue that America took its name from one Amerigo Vespucci, a navigator with the explorer Christopher Columbus.

While that argument rumbles on one thing is certain. It was Amerike who paid another explorer, John Cabot, a pension after his epic voyage across the Atlantic Ocean in 1497. Cabot sailed from the docks in Bristol in search of Japan, China and the East Indies but instead he made landfall at Newfoundland.

His pension came from Port of Bristol funds with Amerike paying it in his role as the King's Customs Officer for the port.

Amerike, who was descended from the Earls of Gwent, was born in Ross-on-Wye. After his marriage he moved to Somerset where he set up home near the market town of Ilchester. Amerike later settled in Bristol which was then the second largest port in England after London. He served as the town's Sheriff and was Chief Customs Collector on three occasions, although this important post was usually held for one year only.

He lived at Lower Court Farm, Long Ashton, a mile or two south of the city. His daughter and her husband, John Brook, are buried in St Mary Redcliffe church.

Isaac Arrowsmith

(?—1871)

It might be hard to believe, but some of the world's classic books were printed in a cellar underneath Bristol city centre.

The family printing business that Isaac Arrowsmith set up was based in a building on the corner of Quay Street and Colston Avenue and the cellar was his print shop.

It was here that books like Anthony Hope's *The Prisoner of Zenda*, George Crossmith's *Diary of A Nobody* and Jerome K Jerome's *Three Men In A Boat* rolled off the press. Arrowsmith's were at Quay Street for ninety-seven years until the firm moved to new premises at Ashton Gate.

Isaac Arrowsmith came to Bristol with his family from Worcester where he was a partner in the *Worcester Chronicle* and a founder member of the local typographical society.

His first publication in Bristol was a timetable of steam packets and railway trains, costing a penny, which appeared in 1854. The company went on to publish many books including much Bristoliana. It printed and published its own *Dictionary of Bristol* in 1906, and three large volumes of Nicholls' *Bristol Past and Present*, which still remains a standard reference work for historians.

For many years Arrowsmith's were printers to many well-respected city institutions like Bristol University, Bristol Waterworks and the building firm of Cowlin's.

The firm always stayed a family business but unfortunately a large chunk of Bristol history came to an end in 2006 when the firm went into administration.

Sir Herbert Ashman

(1854—1914)

Councillor Herbert Ashman had the unique distinction of being the last Mayor of Bristol and the city's first Lord Mayor.

The list of Mayors is impressively long, dating back to 1216. It came to an end when Queen Victoria granted the city a Lord Mayoralty in 1889. She also said that Bristol's First Citizen should be styled 'The Right Honourable' — one of only five Lord Mayors in England and Wales who may be addressed in this way.

Cllr Ashman's council colleagues gave him the honour of being first Lord Mayor — on completion of his term of office as Mayor.

Another prestigious honour came his way when Queen Victoria granted him a knighthood. Instead of receiving Cllr Ashman at Buckingham Palace to officially bestow the award on him, Her Majesty carried out the ceremony on the steps of the Old Council House, Corn Street, where councillors held their meetings.

Remarkably, she knighted Cllr Ashman without stepping out of her carriage. Instead she leant out of her horse-drawn landau and dubbed him on the shoulder with a sword that she had borrowed from a member of the royal entourage. This was the last personal conferment of a knighthood that Queen Victoria made before she died two years later.

After he retired as a councillor, Sir Herbert was elected to the city's aldermanic bench. He was one of the earliest advocates of a greater Bristol, an idea that still surfaces from time to time for discussion.

Herbert Ashman joined his father's firm of leather merchants and importers when he was fifteen years old. Seven years later with his brother he founded his own leather business that included making driving belts for most kinds of machinery.

The firm had a warehouse in Broadmead which in 1932 became the birthplace of the *Bristol Evening Post*. This was the newspaper's home until 1974 when its present headquarters, a purpose-built press hall and offices was opened in Temple Way.

John Atyeo

(1932—1993)

There can't be many footballers who stay with one club throughout their career. John Atyeo, though, was one of the few who did just that.

He had played as an amateur for the Wiltshire team Westbury United and was signed by Bristol City from under the noses of league champions Portsmouth.

Atyeo, who had turned out several times as an amateur for the south coast club, joined Bristol City in 1951 when he was nineteen, although it was on a part-time basis. He insisted that he would only sign a full-time contract after he had qualified as a surveyor.

The signing of Atyeo was unusual when compared with the razzmatazz of the press conferences that are called today when any football club takes on a new player. City's chairman at the time, Bristol businessman Harry Dolman travelled to Dilton Marsh in Wiltshire to meet Atyeo's father in order get the signature he wanted.

Atyeo played at centre forward and stayed with City for fifteen years, playing in 645 games. He put the ball into the net on 350 occasions, both in football league and cup matches. It is a club record that still stands today. Atyeo was also capped by England six times from 1955 to 1957.

He prided himself in never being booked or sent off during his career, and was idolised by thousands of fans who affectionately nicknamed him 'Gentle John'.

There were offers for Atyeo to sign for Tottenham Hotspur, Chelsea and Liverpool, but he shunned the glamour of some of the country's top clubs, preferring to stay loyal to the West Country side that gave him his big break.

He hung up his boots for the last time in 1966 and went on to teach maths at a school in Warminster for twenty years.

Atyeo died in 1993 from a heart attack. However, he is not forgotten at Bristol City, where one of the stands at the club's Ashton Gate stadium is named after him.

Edward Hodges Baily

(1788—1867)

Edward Hodges Baily lightened the routine of lessons for his classmates at Bristol Grammar School by modelling wax portraits of them. It was an interest he probably picked up from his father, a well-known carver of ships' figureheads in the city.

When he left school at the age of fourteen Baily was placed in a merchant's office but stayed only two years before moving to London. He was soon introduced to the celebrated sculptor John Flaxman, who became the first Professor of Sculpture at the Royal Academy, and worked in his studio for seven years.

Before his twentieth birthday Baily's skill had already been recognised by the Society of Arts who honoured him with a prize. A few years later the Royal Academy granted him full membership.

Edward Baily put himself amongst the front rank of sculptors with his marble statue *Eve at the Fountain* which can still be seen at Bristol Museum and Art Gallery.

He became a prolific sculptor carving busts and statues of leading figures of the day, from politicians to poets and from painters to scientists. Although many of them can still be seen in churches and public squares across the country, the name of Baily is hardly remembered today.

In Bristol he was responsible for the frieze above the entrance to the Freemason's Hall in Park Street and the statue *Justice* above the Old Council House in Corn Street. The seventeen foot high statue of Admiral Nelson standing on its lofty perch at the top of Nelson's Column in Trafalgar Square, London, is also the work of Baily.

Baily, who was born at Downend, spent most of his life in London. He married when he was eighteen and became the father of two sons and two daughters. When he died at the age of seventy-nine one newspaper obituary described him as 'the greatest of modern sculptors'.

Banksy

(1974—)

Bristol's — and Britain's — most celebrated graffiti artist. Although we know he was born in the city and educated here we don't know his real name or where he lives, for Banksy jealously guards his identity. Several national newspapers have claimed they know who he is but Banksy has never risen to the bait.

He started creating graffiti when he was a teenager, quickly becoming part of the Bristol artistic scene, using stencils to 'tag' his name on artwork across the city.

Banksy's work not only appears on buildings in Bristol and London, but at other locations around the world too. Pieces of his art have also been found hanging in London's Tate Modern, the New York Museum of Modern Art, and other major art centres in America, though no one has seen them being hung! His version of a primitive cave painting, depicting a human figure hunting wildlife while pushing a shopping cart, was found hanging in the British Museum. On another occasion he was reported to have painted nine images on the Palestinian side of the Israeli West Bank barrier including one of a ladder up and over the wall.

Banksy produced the album cover design for the 2003 comeback album *Think Tank* for Britpop band Blur. Apparently, the band's frontman Damon Albarn is a big fan. Some of Banksy's pieces have been bought for hundreds of thousands of pounds by private collectors. Many Hollywood celebrities are among the collectors of his work.

In 2009, with only a few members of staff in the know, Banksy took over Bristol Museum and Art Gallery to stage what was, in effect, a secret exhibition. After museum staff had gone home for the night he replaced many of the artifacts on display with 100 pieces of his own work, including a spray-painted burnt-out ice cream van, sculptures and prints, some of which had never been displayed before. From June to the end of August the *Banksy vs Bristol Museum* exhibition attracted 308,719 visitors, a record for any exhibition at the museum. *The Art Newspaper* reported that it was the 30th most visited exhibition in the world that year.

Banksy has since branched out into the world of films, directing and appearing in *Exit Through the Gift Shop*. Publicity material for the production describes it as a 'documentary' about an eccentric French shopkeeper and an amateur film-maker who attempt to locate and befriend Banksy. The film had its premiere at the Berlin Film Festival before doing the rounds in cinemas. Although Banksy appears in the film he is careful not to let the camera see his face, thus preserving his anonymity.

Anton Bantock

(1933—)

The University of Withywood must be the smallest and most unusual seat of learning in the world. Its campus has no spires, gothic towers, college chapels, ancient traditions or even academic hoods and gowns.

But it does have a Latin motto, well-established curricula and visiting lecturers, and hundreds of students have passed through its portals.

Historian Anton Bantock created the university in 1988 after taking early retirement from a local secondary school where he had taught for twenty-seven years. He had a small extension built to his bungalow home at Withywood, on Bristol's southern edge, to house his collections of books that had inspired his pupils. This became known as the library and led to the opening of the University of Withywood.

Since then Anton Bantock's home has been used almost continuously for events, lectures and exhibitions. Varied and interesting lectures by visiting speakers and projects in which local people can participate have been provided by Anton Bantock. On many occasions the bungalow's small rooms have been packed to capacity.

The university is a registered charity with all monies raised from donations, lectures and exhibitions going into a sponsorship fund. It provides around £15,000 a year to help educate young people in Third World countries.

Anton Bantock has been made an MBE for his services to the community, especially education in south Bristol.

William Barrett

(1727—1789)

One of Bristol's earliest historians, arguably the first, was William Barrett, a surgeon and obstetrician who lived in the city for thirty years. He was born in Wiltshire but moved to Bristol after passing his medical exams when he was twenty-two years old.

Barrett divided his life between the medical profession and antiquarian research. After his wife died he devoted much of his time to researching and writing the first comprehensive history of Bristol. A lot of the information he gathered came from records collected from families that he visited as a doctor, including the gentry, councillors and successful merchants.

He turned his research into thirty-six chapters on the origins of Bristol, up to its development in the 18th century, giving it the title *History and Antiquities of Bristol*. Barrett described the work as an amusement rather than a labour or study. It was published in 1789 but some of his critics derided the book as it included information from the boy poet Thomas Chatterton which had been fabricated.

Barrett died five months after publication of the book while visiting his son, a priest, at High Ham in Somerset.

Dr Thomas Beddoes

(1760—1808)

One of the country's most unusual laboratories was opened by Dr Thomas Beddoes, a medical man and a scientist, who was interested in gases. He had studied medicine in London and Edinburgh and was a Reader in Chemistry at Cambridge University, before settling in Bristol where he opened his grandly named Pneumatic Institution.

It was here that controversial experiments to find a cure for such diseases as tuberculosis, asthma and dropsy were conducted with patients inhaling wind from cows.

He imported frogs from France for his experiments into the cause and cure of consumption. When thousands of frogs escaped from their container at the docks, protestors marched on Dr Beddoes' home.

He initially set up his laboratory in a Georgian house in Hope Square, Hotwells, but later moved into a corner house in fashionable Dowry Square, just down the hill.

Although it appears that there was no shortage of patients willing to be guinea pigs in search of a cure, Dr Beddoes' Institution in Dowry Square had a short life — no more than three years — and was not successful in its aims. Two members of his staff were Peter Roget, who later compiled his famous Thesaurus, and Humphry Davy. It was while he was working for Dr Beddoes that Davy discovered nitrous oxide, or laughing gas, which was later used as an anaesthetic.

After the Institution closed in 1801 Dr Beddoes, who wrote on medical, social and political matters, continued to live at Rodney Place, Clifton, where he hosted many gatherings of literary society.

He married Anna Edgeworth, sister of Maria, a novelist who was living nearby. His son, Thomas Lovell Beddoes, who was born at Rodney Place in 1803, became a Romantic poet and physiologist.

Tony Benn (former MP)

(1925—)

The election of Anthony (Tony) Neil Wedgwood Benn as Member of Parliament for Bristol South East in 1950 opened a colourful chapter in the history of British politics. He held the seat for the Labour Party in a by-election caused by the resignation of Stafford Cripps through ill health. At the time Benn was the youngest member of the House of Commons.

Ten years later though, on the death of his father, Viscount Stansgate, Benn had to stand down. The law at the time made him ineligible to serve in the House of Commons as he had inherited a peerage.

While he vigorously campaigned to get the law changed a by-election for his Bristol seat was called. Although he had no chance of returning to Westminster as an MP Benn stood for election coming top of the poll. However, the Conservative Party candidate, Malcolm St Clair, was declared Member of Parliament.

Two years later the Peerage Act became law enabling Benn to officially renounce his title. Malcolm St Clair resigned the seat and another by-election was held, this time without any official Conservative Party candidate standing. Benn again came top of the poll with an Independent Conservative coming second.

During his time in the House of Commons Benn held various offices including those of Postmaster General and Minister of Technology. He represented Bristol South East until the 1983 General Election when constituency boundary changes helped to bring about his defeat. However, he was back in parliament at the next election, winning the Chesterfield seat.

Tony Benn retired at the 2001 General Election quirkily saying that he wished to leave Westminster to 'spend more time in politics'. He has published his diaries, political books and pamphlets and has devised his own touring one-man show.

In recognition of his service to Bristol the city council made him an Honorary Freeman in 2003.

Roger Bennett

(1935—2005)

This newspaper journalist turned broadcaster presented BBC Radio Bristol's early morning news programme for twenty-nine years making him the longest serving breakfast presenter in the country.

Roger Bennett was so popular that when he died his listeners raised funds for a permanent memorial to him: a stained glass panel in St Mary Redcliffe Church.

He won many awards, including the Sony Radio Presenter of the Year, Local Broadcaster of the Year and Sony Gold Achievement Award for dedication to local radio. An honorary Masters degree was conferred on him by Bristol University.

Aside from broadcasting, he was well known as a jazz musician and regularly played the saxophone with the West Country legend Acker Bilk. In the 1950's he helped found the Blue Notes band which still has a weekly club night for their followers.

Roger Bennett was passionately proud of his Bristol roots. He was brought up in the St Andrews area and went to the local Sefton Park Primary School before moving on to Bristol Grammar School.

Before joining the BBC, Roger Bennett worked for the *Bristol Evening Post* as its Chief Reporter. His father, Bob, ran the paper's Pillar Box Club for younger readers and was also well known as a cartoonist.

Frank and Aldo Berni

(Frank 1903—2000 and Aldo 1909—1997)

Little could Frank and Aldo Berni have dreamt that when they opened their first steak and chips restaurant in Bristol in the austere post-war years, that they would change a nation's eating habits.

Customers of Berni's didn't have to worry about understanding a menu written in French. The food on offer at all the firm's branches was the same with plaice as an alternative to steak. There was also a limited choice of starters and sweets with the bill coming to 7s 6d (the equivalent of 37.5p in present currency). The Berni brothers had been running the well respected and up-market Horts Restaurant in Broad Street, since 1943 before opening the steak bar twelve years later. They took over the council-owned Rummer Hotel and Dining Rooms in the heart of St Nicholas Market which quickly became one of the city's Bristol's most popular restaurants.

A chain of Berni Inns soon opened across the city in historic pubs like the Llandoger Trow and the Hole in The Wall. Soon the Berni menu was appearing at inns across the country as the brothers started taking over pub after pub.

The brothers were much involved in the day-to-day running of their business with Frank Berni as chairman who also kept his eye on the purse while Aldo was very much the front-of-house man making sure the customers were happy.

In 1970 the brothers, who were born in Italy, sold their business of 147 inns for £14 million to another catering group, Grand Metropolitan. Twenty years later it was on the market again with the Whitbread brewing group the buyer this time. The new owners dispensed with the Berni Inns trade name in favour of Beefeater Pubs.

Aldo died in 1997 and Frank, who was 96, died in 2000. A third brother, Marco, who had his own chain of restaurants, died in 1998.

Sir John Betjeman

(1906—1984)

A Londoner by birth, John Betjeman had a special love for the West Country, in particular Bristol. He spent a few months in Clifton as a young man and said the suburb was 'Bristol's biggest surprise'. Later he wrote two poems about Bristol and described it as 'the most beautiful, interesting and distinguished city in England'.

He frequently spent much time here making architectural programmes for the BBC and HTV, the old West Country independent broadcaster. His was the last voice heard on HTV's predecessor Television Wales and West (TWW) when it lost its franchise. John Betjeman sat in a corner of a studio reading a poem called *Come to an End*.

He was the most influential protestor at a public inquiry about a plan to build a modern hotel extension in the Avon Gorge, a couple of hundred yards from the Clifton Suspension Bridge. John Betjeman lined up with other objectors to give evidence to the Inquiry Inspector at a lengthy hearing in Bristol. He was delighted when the hotel was later shelved.

Although best known as a poet, Sir John Betjeman — he was knighted in 1969 — had many jobs ranging from teaching to working on an architectural magazine before taking up the pen full time. He was made Poet Laureate in 1972, a position he held until his death twelve years later.

Ernest Bevin

(1881—1951)

Farmer's boy to Minister of the Crown — it sounds unbelievable but that, in brief, is the life story of Ernest Bevin.

He left school when he was just eleven years old and went to work as a farm labourer in the Exmoor village of Winsford where he was born.

Two years later he was in Bristol washing dishes and peeling potatoes at a hotel. A variety of other jobs followed including grocer's errand boy, van boy and conductor on the new electric trams that were introduced to Bristol in 1894.

It wasn't long before Ernest Bevin took an interest in local politics and was appointed secretary of the Bristol Right to Work Committee. He was an organiser for the dockers' union and quickly became an impassioned champion of its members.

By 1922 nearly three dozen trades unions had been merged into the massive Transport and General Workers Union. Ernest Bevin was appointed its General Secretary, a role that was his for almost two decades.

In 1940 he became Minister of Labour and National Service in Winston Churchill's coalition government and was appointed Foreign Secretary in the Labour Government of 1945—1951. Ill health forced him to retire in March 1951 and he died a month later.

The pirate Blackbeard, from an engraving attributed to James Basire, after a picture by Joseph Nicholls.

Blackbeard

(c1680—1718)

This was the most notorious pirate in the history of seafaring who is said to have lived in the Redcliffe area where he was known as Edward Teach (or Tach).

With a beard that almost covered his face it is said that just the sight of him would strike terror into the hearts of his victims. A big man, he added to his menacing appearance by wearing a crimson coat, two swords at his waist, and bandoleers stuffed with numerous pistols and knives across his chest.

His days of piracy were centred on the Atlantic and the Caribbean where he captured scores of ships. First, the vessels were cleared of any valuables and then set alight. One of them was a French ship, *The Concorde*, which he converted to suit his own taste, arming it with forty guns and renaming it *Queen Anne's Revenge*.

It was off Carolina that Blackbeard met his grisly end during a skirmish at sea when the crew of two naval ships caught up with him. By all accounts Blackbeard was shot five times, stabbed more than twenty, and decapitated with his head being hung on the ship's rigging. His corpse was unceremoniously tossed overboard.

Elizabeth Blackwell

(1821—1910)

The sheer determination and doggedness of Elizabeth Blackwell opened the field of medicine to women in the face of strong male prejudice. Her family's Quaker beliefs — that all men and women should be treated equally — meant she was able to become the first woman in the United Kingdom to graduate as a doctor.

Elizabeth Blackwell, one of nine daughters of Samuel Blackwell, a sugar refiner, spent most of her childhood in the Counterslip and St Paul's districts. When she was eleven years old her father moved the family to America where he set up a refinery in New York.

When he died penniless six years later, Elizabeth helped support the family by teaching, although she devoted much of her spare time to studying medicine using text books borrowed from friends. Her attempts to gain admission to medical schools were rebuffed by the all male staff and students. Her perseverance paid off, for she was eventually accepted into Geneva Medical College, New York. In January 1849 Elizabeth Blackwell graduated with a medical degree and came top of her class.

She found work in a hospital in Paris and later joined the staff of St Bartholomew's Hospital, London, before returning to America where she founded a hospital in New York staffed by women only.

Elizabeth Blackwell eventually moved back to Britain for good and was the first woman to be enrolled on the British Medical Register. With Florence Nightingale she set up the Women's Medical College and taught at the newly-established London School of Medicine for Women. Her passion for her work was such that she did not retire until she was eighty-six years old.

George Braikenridge

(1775—1856)

This 19th century merchant devoted his long retirement of thirty-six years to collecting everything connected with Bristol. He scoured the city for china, old documents, old newspapers and coins, which he kept in a museum at his home in Brislington.

George Braikenbridge is best known for preserving the city's visual history with more than 1,400 paintings and drawings. They provide an invaluable record of buildings and streets dating back to the thirteenth century. Many have since been bombed, demolished in the name of development or altered beyond recognition.

He commissioned all the famous of artists of his day to record city scenes including the wartercolourist Samuel Jackson and T L S Rowbotham. Both came from the group of amateur and professional artists known as the Bristol School. Nearly forty artists are represented in what has become known as the Braikenbridge collection.

People helped Braikenridge by giving him paintings and drawings, and he also bought them from bookshops.

When George Braikenbridge died many of the items he'd collected were sold at London auction houses, but he bequeathed his Bristol paintings to the City Museum and Art Gallery. To this day they are still consulted by historians and lovers of art.

Dr Richard Bright

(1789—1858)

Banker's son Richard Bright, who was born in Queen Square, is regarded as the founder of modern renal medicine.

He studied medicine in London, Edinburgh and Germany before joining the staff of Guy's Hospital, London, where he made an impression with his many clinical and pathological observations. His findings on a kidney disease, which was named after him, were published in 1827.

Shortly after Queen Victoria came to the throne in 1837 Dr Bright was appointed Royal Physician Extraordinary.

He had a family home at Ham Green, North Somerset, which later became Ham Green Hospital where the first renal unit in the Bristol region was set up.

Reverend Thomas Broughton

(1704—1774)

This one-time vicar of St Mary Redcliffe seems to have been best known for being a friend of the composer Handel, who, according to an old guide book, was a regular visitor to Mr Broughton's vicarage.

However, despite extensive searches Handel scholars and historians have never been able to unearth any documentary evidence of visits to Bristol by the composer.

But we do know that Mr Broughton himself was especially interested in music and wrote the lyrics for some of Handel's compositions, including the musical drama *Hercules*. This secular work had its premiere at the King's Theatre in London's Haymarket in 1745.

Mr Broughton, a clergyman's son, was educated at Eton and Cambridge and was a man of considerable talents, being an author, translator, composer and lyricist. He published numerous biographical and miscellaneous works including a *Dictionary of Religions* and translated *Don Quixote* from the French into English.

He was Redcliffe's vicar from 1744 until his death thirty years later. His tomb is beneath the Handel window in Redcliffe church which is unusual in that eight passages from the Messiah are scored into the stained glass. A block of flats near the church is named after him.

Florence Brown

(1899—1981)

Although Bristol has had Mayors and Lord Mayors since 1216, a woman had never held the office of First Citizen until the second half of the twentieth century.

Councillor Florence Brown made civic history when her fellow councillors elected her Lord Mayor by in 1963. Her husband acted as her Consort during her year of office.

Mrs Brown was elected to the city council in 1937 and served on many of its committees including those that looked after the interests of children and education. She was appointed to the aldermanic bench after eighteen years as a councillor.

For much of her working life Mrs Brown was a tobacco stripper at the Wills factory in Bedminster and was a trade union representative there for eleven years. She was awarded the CBE in 1966 and died aged eighty-two.

Louise Brown

(1978—)

The arrival of Louise Brown in the delivery suite made front page headlines from Australia to Zanzibar for she was the world's first test tube baby.

Her parents Lesley and John Brown of Easton, Bristol, had been trying for nine years to start a family but without success. They were invited to take part in the pioneering work of Dr Robert Edwards and Dr Patrick Steptoe at Oldham General Hospital, which involved *in vitro* fertilisation.

As a result Louise was born by caesarean section on 25th July 1978, weighing in at 5lb 12oz. Her birth heralded the start of a scientific revolution with the IVF technique now an accepted part of medical practice.

Four years after Louise's birth Mrs Brown gave birth to her second test tube daughter, this time at Bristol Maternity Hospital.

Meanwhile, Louise has married and set up home in the city with her husband Wesley. The couple became parents themselves in 2006 when Louise gave birth to a son, Cameron, who was conceived naturally.

Despite the ongoing interest in their family shown by newspapers, radio and television stations, especially on anniversaries, Louise and her husband normally opt to stay out of the media spotlight.

*Engineering genius
Isambard Kingdom Brunel.*

Isambard Kingdom Brunel

(1806—1859)

It was an accident that brought the engineering genius Isambard Kingdom Brunel to the West Country. His parents had sent him to Clifton to convalesce after he was involved in an accident whilst working for his father on the Rotherhithe tunnel under the River Thames.

While in Bristol, the young Brunel entered a competition to find a design for a bridge to span the River Avon, linking Clifton on the Bristol bank with Leigh Woods on the Somerset side. The judging panel received twenty-two entries including four from Brunel for different sites. It was one of his designs that the judges eventually accepted.

Work on building the Clifton Suspension Bridge, 245 feet above the River Avon, started in 1831 but was interrupted by a series of financial problems. It took more than thirty years for the landmark project to be completed. Unfortunately, Brunel did not live to see it finished having died five years earlier in 1859.

Whilst the bridge, which he described as his 'darling', was under construction, Brunel accepted the job of engineer of the Great Western Railway. He built all its tunnels, bridges and viaducts and the terminus at Temple Meads.

He went on to design the *SS Great Britain,* the biggest iron ship in the world; and the *Great Western.* Brunel was also responsible for some of the modifications to Bristol's Floating Harbour.

In a busy life he advised on the construction of railways as far away as Australia and East Bengal, and even designed a military hospital for use in the Crimean war.

During the Bristol Riots of 1831 Brunel was enlisted as a special constable helping to save some of the city's silver treasures from the Mansion House (then in Queen Square) which had been looted and destroyed by fire.

His funeral was one of the biggest London had seen at the time. Thousands of people lined the streets as the cortege made its way to Kensal Green cemetery where his father, Sir Marc Isambard Brunel, had been laid to rest ten years previously.

William Budd

(1811—1880)

William Budd, who was given the sobriquet 'The Father of Health', was the sixth of ten children, seven of whom became doctors following in the footsteps of their father, a surgeon in Devon. William was the pioneer of preventative medicine that made Bristol healthy.

He studied medicine in London, Paris and Edinburgh where he was awarded his medical degree. Dr Budd arrived in Bristol in 1841 and set up his practice in Park Street, on the site of what is now a bookshop. The following year he was appointed physician to St Peter's Hospital and at the age of thirty-six was made physician to Bristol Royal Infirmary. He also lectured at Bristol Medical School.

At the Infirmary he was caring for people suffering from typhoid, cholera and typhus. Having survived typhoid fever himself and seen the insanitary slum conditions in which people lived, Dr Budd realised the need for disinfection and prevention of sewage entering the water supply.

He was one of the first directors of the Bristol Waterworks Company and was instrumental in ensuring that the city had a clean water supply. Dr Budd gave evidence to the 1854 Royal Commission on Health in Towns, which marked Bristol down as being the third unhealthiest place in the United Kingdom.

When the cholera epidemic of 1866 reached Bristol, greatly reduced death figures proved that his campaigning had largely won the grim fight to improve the city's health.

He died at the age of sixty-nine and was buried in Arnos Vale Cemetery. The writer of one obituary said: 'To exterminate disease was the passion of his life.' Dr Budd is remembered by a health clinic in Bristol which is named after him. A plaque commemorating his life can be found on the site of his practice in Park Street.

Edmund Burke

(1729—1797)

Irish-born Edmund Burke was Member of Parliament for Bristol from 1774 to 1780, having been asked to stand for election by a number of prominent citizens.

He had become well known for campaigning against the election of MPs who were only friends of the King. Edmund Burke argued for parliament to be made up of people who would be free to argue against the monarch and stand up for ordinary folk. He eventually lost the support of Bristol merchants, though, because of his views on some of the other issues of the day.

Burke used the Bush Inn, a coaching inn on Corn Street, as his election campaign headquarters. It was here that Charles Dickens had Mr Winkle stay in his lovelorn quest for the missing Arabella Allen in *Pickwick Papers*. A bank now stands on the site of the inn.

A quotation from a speech he made in Bristol is carved on the plinth of his bronze statue in Colston Avenue. It simply says: 'I wish to be a member of parliament to have my share of doing good and resisting evil'. The statue is a replica of one in St Stephen's Hall at the Houses of Parliament and was given to the city by WD Wills of the tobacco family.

Sir Billy Butlin

(1899–1980)

His full name was William Heygate Edmund Colborne Butlin, but to thousands of families he was known simply as Billy Butlin the holiday camp king.

Billy Butlin was born in South Africa and arrived in Bristol as a little boy after his mother's first marriage failed and she married a local gas worker. The young Butlin went to St Mary Redcliffe School before emigrating to Canada.

After wartime service with the Canadian army he worked his passage back across the Atlantic to Liverpool, was paid five pounds, and walked 160 miles back to Bristol.

His career in providing family entertainment started when he paid just thirty shillings (£1.50) at Lock's Yard, Bedminster — at the time the winter quarters of fairground folk — for a portable hoop-la stall.

He then toured the West Country fair circuit travelling by train with his portable stall. His first trip was to a fair at Axbridge, between Bristol and Bridgwater. It's said that Billy Butlin gave out prizes more quickly than his rival hoop-la operators and took ten times their profits.

Billy Butlin went from hoop-la stalls to amusement parks and zoos and in 1936 he raised the money to open his first holiday camp at Skegness. It was an immediate success with the public and he was encouraged to open other camps around the country. He was knighted in 1964.

Dame Clara Butt

(1873—1936)

Clara Butt was one of the country's greatest contraltos, of whom it was said that her booming voice, with its amazing range and power could be heard on the other side of the English Channel.

She was born in Southwick, West Sussex, but in 1880 when she was seven her family moved to Bristol where they had several addresses in Totterdown and Southville.

Clara had her first singing lessons at the Bath Road Academy and later performed in concerts at nearly every church hall in the city, later joining the Bristol Festival Chorus. She won a scholarship to the Royal College of Music making her professional debut as Ursula in Arthur Sullivan's cantata *The Golden Legend*.

She went on to become a superstar singer of the Victorian era performing to packed concert halls all over the world, and was often invited to sing at Buckingham Palace and Windsor Castle.

The composer Edward Elgar was so impressed by Clara Butt's talent that he wrote his Sea Pictures especially for her which she first performed at Norwich Festival in 1899. She made several early gramophone records including *Land of Hope and Glory* which became a favourite among her followers.

Although she toured widely in America, Canada, Australia and New Zealand, Clara Butt never forgot the city where she spent her early years. She married the baritone Robert Rumford at Bristol Cathedral in 1900 having turned down the chance of a wedding in St Paul's Cathedral. One newspaper reported that the cathedral's doors were closed when it was 'full to suffocation'. Workers across the city had been given a half day off to mark the occasion.

Queen Victoria sent a gift while Sir Arthur Sullivan, of Gilbert and Sullivan, wrote a special anthem for the wedding ceremony. The city council gave the bride a diamond brooch bearing the initials CB — standing for Clara Butt and City of Bristol.

She was created a Dame in 1920 in recognition of raising thousands of pounds for the Red Cross during the First World War. Clara Butt died at the age of sixty-three from spinal cancer two years after her last concert in Sydney.

John and Sebastian Cabot

(John c1450—c1498 and Sebastian c1477—1557)

Giovanni Caboto — John Cabot to you and me — put Bristol on the world maritime map. It was in 1497 that this explorer from Genoa with his son Sebastian and a crew of eighteen local men set sail from the port, eventually discovering the mainland of America. He had set out, though, hoping to find exotic goods from the Asian continent.

In his small ship, *The Matthew*, Cabot and his intrepid seamen, guided just by the stars, took fifty-two days to cross the Atlantic Ocean before making landfall at Newfoundland on Midsummer's Day.

On Cabot's return to England, King Henry VII granted him a pension which was paid by Richard Amerike, then customs collector for the Port of Bristol. Cabot set sail from Bristol again the following year with a fleet of ships but was never heard of after that.

Bristolians have always taken pride in his voyage of discovery. To mark its 400th anniversary they built a 105-foot-high tower, named after him, on Brandon Hill park. The 500th anniversary in 1997 was celebrated with much enthusiasm with a group of local men recreating Cabot's voyage. Wearing period dress they sailed across the Atlantic in a replica of *The Matthew* which had been built in Bristol docks. It now has a permanent berth in the harbour.

Sebastian Cabot, who is thought to have been born in Bristol, later went to Spain and became a cartographer to Ferdinand, returning to England in 1547. He was made Grand Pilot of England and became the first governor of the Company of Merchant Adventurers of London.

Don Cameron

(1940—)

One man's name is synonymous with ballooning across the world — that of businessman Don Cameron. He has helped to make the sport accessible to all through the prolific production of balloons at his factory, the largest of its kind in the world.

It all began when Don, a balloonist himself, decided to create an event that would draw together like-minded people from around the world. In September 1979 nearly thirty balloonists met for the first ever Bristol Balloon Fiesta. It was organised by Bristol Junior Chamber of Commerce and Shipping and held at Ashton Court estate. Since then it has become an international event with more than one hundred fliers heading for the skies each year.

While still at school in Glasgow Don Cameron, whose hobby was aero-modelling, won a flying scholarship to RAF Hornchurch, London and soon learned to fly a Tiger Moth biplane. He qualified in aero-engineering at Glasgow University and found a job at the old Bristol Aeroplane Company in 1961.

Don Cameron holds many ballooning records and has been awarded gold, silver and bronze medals by the British Royal Aero Club for his achievements. His attempt to make the first Atlantic crossing by balloon in 1978 ended when bad weather forced his craft down in sight of the French coast after 2,000 miles. However, he was the first person to cross the Sahara Desert by hot air balloon as well as the Alps.

He started making balloons in the basement of his home in Bristol, later moving into a nearby church hall. Since then Don has moved the business again, this time to a former print and packaging factory in Bedminster where his staff make balloons of all shapes and sizes, from houses to cars, for both leisure and promotional use.

William Canynges.

*William Canynges: a
medieval merchant prince.*

William Canynges

(1402—1474)

William Canynges the Younger, the third son of John and grandson of William Canynges, was the Richard Branson of his day. He was the biggest ship owner in Bristol, controlling about a quarter of all the shipping in the docks and owning nearly half of the town's vessels.

He was an enterprising merchant with 800 seamen on his books, making him the biggest employer in Bristol. His ships traded with Iceland, France, Spain and the Mediterranean. When relations between England and Denmark became strained he was granted special dispensation by King Christian I to continue sending out ships to Scandanavia and Iceland.

Contemporary chroniclers described Canynges as 'the greatest English merchant of the fifteenth century'.

His wealth enabled him to complete the work of his ancestors in the rebuilding of St Mary Redcliffe church. He is credited with adding the church's magnificent clerestory windows.

He also played a prominent part in the town's civic life, serving twice as Sheriff, twice representing Bristol in parliament and holding the office of Mayor five times.

Canynges was a friend of royalty and entertained the young King Edward IV at his house in Redcliffe Street.

After the death of his wife in 1467 Canynges gave up his worldly possessions to train for the priesthood eventually becoming Dean of Westbury College, Westbury-on-Trym. There are two tomb effigies of Canynges in St Mary Redcliffe. One is very ornate and shows him lying with his wife Joanna while the other shows him in a simple priest's robe.

CARABOO PRINCESS OF JAVASU.

*Princess Caraboo
from an engraving by
Henry Meyer, after a
picture by Edward Bird.*

'Princess Caraboo'

(1791—1864)

One of the strangest characters to stroll through the pages of Bristol's history is the cobbler's daughter who fooled people into thinking that she was a princess from a remote island who'd been kidnapped by pirates, escaped, and made her way to England.

It was in 1817 that this twenty-six year-old wearing a black turban with colourful clothing was found wandering the streets of Almondsbury, north of Bristol. She talked in a language no one could understand. Feeling sorry for her the county magistrate provided accommodation for her at his country mansion.

When she was introduced to a Portugese sailor the woman claimed to be Princess Caraboo of Javasu, an island in the Indian Ocean. Her story was that she had been kidnapped from her home by pirates, held captive on their ship but escaped by jumping overboard into the Bristol Channel and swimming ashore.

The so-called princess danced exotically for the magistrate's friends and even swam naked in a lake. By all accounts she was having a wonderful time until the landlady of a boarding house in Bristol recognised the description of the woman in a newspaper report. She had provided the 'princess' with lodgings some six month earlier.

The ruse which went on for three months was over. Under questioning it transpired that the self-styled princess was really Mary Wilcocks from Devon. Apparently, she adopted the disguise thinking it would make her more interesting.

After being unmasked she set up home in Southville selling leeches. When she died she was buried in a local churchyard.

Mary Carpenter
(1807—1877)

Mary Carpenter was one of the great 19th century pioneers of social reform, best known for her work amongst the poverty-stricken children and young people from the slums in Bristol. Less well known are the visits she made to India in the last ten years of her life to improve the lot of women there.

She was the eldest of six children who came to Bristol from Exeter when their father took up the post of minister at the Unitarian Free Church in Lewins Mead. Astonished by the appalling conditions in the crowded courtyards and alleys, Mary Carpenter was inspired to open a Ragged School for what were then known as 'gutter children'.

She ran another school at Kingswood and set up the world's first reformatory school for girls in the Red Lodge, Park Row. This was financed by the widow of Lord Byron and Mary Carpenter worked here for two decades.

After meeting the Indian social reformer Raja Ramohun Roy who was on a visit to Bristol, Mary Carpenter travelled to India four times to help children, women and prisoners there.

She died aged seventy and was buried at Arnos Vale cemetery. A memorial plaque in Bristol Cathedral bears an inscription referring to Mary Carpenter as 'foremost among the founders of reformatory and industrial schools in this city and the realm.' It praises her for 'taking to heart the grievous lot of oriental women' and says she awakened an 'active interest in their education and training for serious duties.'

John Carr

(c1539—1586)

Merchant John Carr's wealth came from selling soap at a penny a pound which was made at his factories in Bristol and London. He was also the owner of houses in Bristol and North Somerset.

Shortly before his death at the age of fifty-two, John Carr drew up a will with detailed instructions as to how his fortune should be distributed. A substantial legacy was earmarked to set up a school for orphans and poor boys in Bristol. He wanted it to be modelled on Christ's Hospital, London, which was founded to help fatherless children and those from poor homes.

Carr's bequest led to the founding of Queen Elizabeth's Hospital with Queen Elizabeth I granting the school its charter four years after Carr's death. This confirmed its title and rights and also made the Mayor and commonalty of Bristol 'patrons, guiders and governors of the said hospital for ever.'

Carr's school, or hospital, opened with just a dozen boys in the mansion of Gaunts House in Denmark Street near College Green. Today it occupies a mock Tudor building put up on Brandon Hill in 1847.

For more than four centuries the school's distinctive uniform of dark cloak, yellow stockings and buckle shoes worn by boarders, was a familiar sight on the city's streets. However, with the number of boarders dwindling the school ceased enrolling them in 2008.

Rt Rev Richard Cartwright

(1913—2009)

At a time when church fundraising was far from imaginative and limited to jumble sales and donations from worshippers, the Rev Richard Cartwright had far bigger ideas.

He said it was unthinkable that St Mary Redcliffe, allegedly described by Elizabeth l as 'the fairest, goodliest and most famous parish church in England' should be allowed to decay.

Richard Cartwright gathered together many distinguished people to lead an international appeal in 1961. Among them were John Betjeman, later to become Poet Laureate, the Duke of Beaufort and leading businessmen in Bristol.

As part of the appeal he made several lecture tours of America, in one speech declaring:

> *I am sure that in Bristol there is a tremendous amount of goodwill. I am not a bit frightened about that. But to try to get such a huge sum from Bristol alone is a bit much. However, I think that through the length of Britain and in the United States of America too, there are many people who love St Mary Redcliffe and are grateful for what has come from it.*

On one visit alone he covered some 17,000 miles in five weeks, preaching and giving talks about Redcliffe. The support from many Americans led to the furnishing of St John's Chapel, under the church's tower, also known today as the American Chapel.

The restoration was paid for and completed by 1965 with the stonemasons carving a head of Mr Cartwright on the tower. To mark the end of the restoration he organised a special service which was attended by Princess Margaret.

Richard Cartwright was no stranger at meeting royalty. He escorted the Queen around the church when she made her first official visit to Bristol as monarch in 1956.

He left Redcliffe after twenty years on appointment as Bishop of Plymouth. After his retirement to Exeter in 1982 he was for a while Assistant Bishop of Truro.

William Champion

(1710–1789)

William Champion pioneered the working of brass and zinc at his 18th century works on the rural outskirts of Bristol having moved from the centre of the city because of complaints about pollution.

He was a skilled metallurgist who invented a new method of smelting zinc, built his own smelter and installed a modern steam engine at Warmley. Among his financial backers were several wealthy Bristol families, the Goldneys and the Harfords.

In his heyday Champion was employing around 2,000 people, some of them children. Apart from smelting copper and brass they made everything from pots and pans to pins.

Champion turned his mind to building a dock at Hotwells. His Great Dock was capable of holding up to *thirty-six* of the largest ships which came into the Port of Bristol! However, it was never a successful venture and five years after building it Champion sold it to the Society of Merchant Venturers. From then on it was known as Merchants Docks. The dock has long been filled in and the Rownham Mead housing development now stands on the site.

Champion also came up with a scheme to turn the docks into a floating harbour by installing lock gates across the River Avon near the point where the River Frome joined it. However, his scheme was not favoured by the port authorities who claimed it was too costly. Instead, they opted for a similar idea put up by the leading civil engineer William Jessop.

N.C. Branwhite, del.ᵗ   W.J. Edwards, Sculp.

CHATTERTON.

"THE MARVELLOUS BOY WHO PERISHED IN HIS PRIDE." SOUTHEY.

From a picture in the possession of
George Weare Braikenridge, Esq.
of
Broomwell House, Brislington.

*Thomas Chatterton,
the boy poet.*

Thomas Chatterton

(1752—1770)

Thomas Chatterton, the 'boy poet', is more famous for dying young after taking arsenic in a garret than for the verses he wrote. He cut short his life three months before his eighteenth birthday in despair because his poetic genius had gone unrecognised.

Chatterton was born in a house that still stands opposite St Mary Redcliffe church and wrote his first verses at the age of ten. Some of his work appeared in a Bristol newspaper a year later.

He spent many hours in the Muniment Room of Redcliffe church fascinated by scraps of ancient charters and manuscripts he found. From these 'discoveries' Chatterton taught himself to write in medieval style and created an imaginary character — a monk he called Thomas Rowley.

Chatterton claimed that Rowley had lived two centuries earlier and had written the poetry that he supposedly found. One leading critic acclaimed the verses to be the greatest literary 'find' of the century.

However, Chatterton's fraud was eventually exposed and he became known as a forger. He moved to London where he took arsenic and was buried in a pauper's grave.

It was only after his death that Chatterton was recognised as a genius with William Wordsworth describing him as the 'marvellous boy'. Dr Johnson and Boswell visited St Mary Redcliffe church after Chatterton's death to see where the supposed Rowley manuscripts were found.

The Clarke Family

According to a national newspaper report Giles Clarke (1953—) once worked as a penniless goatherd in Damascus, a far cry from the high-flying business life he now leads.

Mr Clarke was working on the land to pay his way through college but was said to be pondering on the fortune to be made from wine.

After completing his studies, Giles Clarke worked in London as an investment banker. He later bought from receivership the assets of Majestic Wine Warehouse which he turned into a money-spinning chain and sold eight years later for £15 million.

Mr Clarke has since been involved in many other headline-making business ventures. He founded the chain of Pet City stores, later selling it for £110 million, and built up Safestore PLC into the country's third largest self-storage company. It was sold for a reported £4 million.

Apart the world of high finance Mr Clarke is involved with many charitable causes in Bristol and is chairman of the England and Wales Cricket Board.

He comes from a family whose roots are deeply entrenched in Bristol soil. His father Charles (1926—2003) was a senior partner in the long established law firm Osborne Clarke; his uncle Jack was a founding director of HTV, the ITV station serving Wales and the West Country; and mother Stella (1936—) was a governor of the BBC, and former Chairman of Bristol Magistrates.

Stella was the first woman to head the governing body of a British university when she was elected chairman of the Council of Bristol University in 1987. It was a post she held for ten years. By the time of that appointment Mrs Clarke had already been active in public life for more than three decades starting as a local councillor at the age of twenty-three.

She has also served as Deputy Lord Lieutenant of Bristol and Vice Lord Lieutenant, which involved her in planning royal visits to the city and welcoming members of the royal family on their arrival.

Samuel Taylor Coleridge

(1772—1832)

Samuel Taylor Coleridge first came to Bristol in the early 1790s as a friend of Robert Southey, whom he met at Cambridge University where he was studying to become a church minister, following in his father's footsteps.

In Bristol, he gave lectures at Unitarian chapels, wrote articles and edited the radical Christian journal *The Watchman*, which was launched in the Rummer pub in 1795.

Coleridge and Southey married two sisters, Sarah and Edith Fricker from Westbury-on-Trym, within a month of each other at St Mary Redcliffe church in 1795.

The Coleridges first went to live at Clevedon but later returned to Bristol staying at various addresses including Kingsdown where their son Hartley was born. He too, became a poet. The family then moved to Nether Stowey before settling in the Lake District.

Coleridge was friendly with William Wordsworth and in 1798 a Bristol publisher Joseph Cottle brought out their book *Lyrical Ballads*, a collection of poems written in popular ballad and lyrical form. They included Coleridge's famous poems *The Rime of the Ancient Mariner* and *The Nightingale*.

AEJ Collins

(1886—1914)

Cricket thrives on bizarre and brilliant achievements, probably none more so than that of a Clifton College schoolboy.

It was in 1889 that thirteen year-old Arthur EJ Collins strode out on to the crease at the school's cricket field, known as The Close, for a junior house match. Remarkably, he stayed at the wicket for five days during which time he scored 628 runs not out.

This was a score that not only put him into the pages of The Times but also those of Wisden, the cricketers' 'bible', and the Guinness Book of Records. It is a score that has never been equalled or surpassed either by amateur or professional cricketers anywhere in the world.

When he left Clifton College, Collins went into the army at Woolwich Barracks where he scored a century in a match against Sandhurst. He was also awarded a bronze medal for boxing.

Collins was commissioned into the Royal Engineers and after a posting in India was sent to France with the British Expeditionary Force. He was killed on the Western Front in the first year of the First World War.

His cricketing skill is still remembered at Clifton College by a commemorative plaque at The Close. On the 100th anniversary of Collins' record-breaking score the college staged a special match with players dressed in Victorian kit.

Edward Colston

(1636—1721)

It is almost impossible to be unaware of the name and fame of the Bristolian regarded as one of the city's greatest benefactors. It seems that the name of Edward Colston is everywhere. Schools, hospitals, charities, almshouses, a dozen streets, a concert hall and a multi-storey office block are named after him. There's a statue of him, appropriately, in Colston Avenue, and stained glass windows in several churches commemorate his life and work.

Colston, who was born in Temple Street, left his mark on the city by giving away some £80,000 during his lifetime, a vast fortune in the 18th century. With his wealth he endowed almshouses, schools and charities and restored churches in the city.

He was a prominent sugar merchant with interests in the Caribbean island of St Kitts, and with others set up a sugar refinery near Christmas Steps. Colston was also a slave trader — an activity now rightly viewed with much abhorrence but which at the time was perfectly legal. He was a member of the Court of Assistants to the London based Royal African Company, which held the monopoly on the slave trade until 1698.

There is a rather engaging tale that on returning from the West Indies one of his ships sprang a leak but a dolphin forced itself into the hole, stopping the leak and thereby saving one of Colston's most valuable cargoes. Whatever the truth of that story, the Colston arms to this day consist of two dolphins facing each other.

The benefactions of Colston, who died when he was eighty-five, are far from forgotten in Bristol. Four charities — the Colston, Anchor, Grateful and Dolphin societies — formed in the 18th century in his memory, are still raising funds for good causes. On November 13th each year Colston's birthday is remembered by members of the societies who process in top hats and tails through the business quarter of the city to lay a wreath on his ornate tomb in All Saints church on Corn Street. Girls from Colston's School decorate his statue with chrysanthemums, his favourite flower.

Russ Conway

(1925—2000)

Trevor Herbert Stanford was better known as honky-tonk pianist Russ Conway, whose playing style and own compositions took him to the number one spot in the pop charts. He did not have any formal tuition but listened to his mother at the keyboard.

After serving with the Royal Navy during the Second World War — he was awarded the Distinguished Service Medal for gallantry in minesweeping in the Aegean and Mediterranean Seas — followed by five years in the Merchant Marine Service, Russ decided on a career in show business.

He became accompanist to many star singers including Gracie Fields, vocalist Dorothy Squires, Denis Lotis and Joan Regan.

But it wasn't long before Russ was making his own records and having his own television series as well as topping the bill at the London Palladium. He had a string of hits from 1957 onwards — including a jaunty number *Side Saddle*, which spent twelve weeks at number one and stayed in the Top 20 for more than seven months.

During a showbiz career of more than forty years Russ Conway sold more than thirty million records. To mark his success the music industry honoured him with five gold, two platinum and two silver discs.

Russ Conway was born in Southville in a house overlooking the New Cut. Despite his worldwide fame he never lost his love for his native city, often returning to visit relatives and for television, radio and concert appearances.

His funeral service at St Mary Redcliffe Church ended with a recording of *Side Saddle* being played.

Dr Beryl Corner
(1912—2007)

Half a century before women talked of breaking through the so-called glass ceiling to get to the top in their careers, Beryl Corner had already achieved this. The Bristol-born doctor was the first consultant paediatrician in the South West — in the face of male prejudice — to become a national pioneer in the care of newborn children.

She is perhaps best known for her role in the birth of the world's first natural quadruplets — Frances, Elizabeth, Jennifer and Bridget Good — by Caesarean section at Southmead Hospital in 1948. They all survived to adulthood and Dr Corner kept in touch with them throughout her life.

Dr Corner was born in Henleaze and went to Redland High School, later becoming vice president and chairwoman of its council. When she was seventeen she became a student at the Royal Free Hospital, London. After training she found jobs at several hospitals in the capital and by 1936 was back in Bristol to join the staff of the Bristol Royal Hospital for Sick Children, then on St Michael's Hill.

A year later, despite what she called 'strong male prejudice', Dr Corner was appointed the first consultant paediatrician in the region. She set up the country's second premature baby unit in Bristol.

Even in her later years Dr Corner attended as many lectures and conferences on child health as she could to update her knowledge of neonatal care. She was a founder member of the Neonatal Society and the first woman to be elected to the British Paediatric Association.

In a busy life Dr Corner also found time to get involved with many voluntary organisations across Bristol. She was a magistrate, played the violin in a church choir, was a member of the Bristol Music Club and supported the Friends of Bristol Art Gallery. She also travelled widely and took an interest in photography.

Joseph Cottle

(1770—1855)

Joseph Cottle has gone down in literary history as the first person to publish the works of Coleridge, Wordsworth and Southey. He offered them thirty guineas for the copyright of their poems and in 1798 published *Lyrical Ballads*.

It is said that by the time he was twenty-one, Bristol-born Cottle had read more than 1,000 books. He set up in business as a bookseller and publisher on the corner of High Street and Corn Street. Cottle was also an author and penned a memoir of Coleridge.

He put up the money for Coleridge's wedding ring when he married Sarah Fricker. A month later Cottle lent Robert Southey money for the wedding licence and ring when he married Sarah's sister, Elizabeth.

Joseph Cottle was buried at Arnos Vale Cemetery.

Robin Cousins

(1957—)

Robin Cousins fell in love with ice skating when he was still at junior school. By the time he was nine years old he was used to rising at an early hour and being taken from his home at Sea Mills to the ice rink in the centre of Bristol.

Such was his enthusiasm for skating that he became a familiar face at the Silver Blades rink, putting in several hours practice before going to school. He quickly distinguished himself with his high jumps and spins. By the time he was twelve Robin had collected his first national title as a novice.

At fifteen years old Robin Cousins was junior champion and had made his international debut. He represented Great Britain as an amateur for eight years and won the annual National Senior Championships for three years running.

Robin's trophy cabinet was already groaning with cups and medals as he went on to win the World Free Skating Championship gold medal three times. He sealed his amateur career by taking European Championship gold, and the gold medal in the 1980 Winter Olympics at Lake Placid, America, for figure skating. He was twenty-two years old at the time.

Robin Cousins then started a professional career which has taken him to the West End stage and on tour with his own ice company. Another aspect of his work sees him producing, starring in, or choreographing international television ice shows.

Tom Cribb

(1781—1848)

Tom Cribb was one of the country's most famous bare-knuckle prize fighters who was only defeated once in thirty major fights. He was born in Hanham, the fourth of ten children, and at the age of thirteen had gone to London in search of work. At first he was apprenticed to a bell-hanger but moved on to be a porter in a coal warehouse at Wapping Docks. Cribb was nicknamed 'The Black Diamond', a reference to his work in the coal trade.

The record books show that Cribb's single defeat was at the hands of George Nicholls in 1805, and that was in the fifty-second round. When he defeated the American boxer Tom Molineaux, the centre of London was brought to a standstill with the huge number of Cribb's followers who wanted to pay tribute to the champion. It was a title the dedicated Tom Cribb held for ten years. It is said that he would walk up to a hundred miles to get his weight down before a match.

Cribb regularly fought at pubs in Bristol including the Hatchet in Frogmore Street where a boxing ring was set up at the rear. St James Fair in Bristol and Bath Races were other popular venues for his fights. His spectators included the Tsar of Russia and the King of Prussia. His fame meant that portrait artists were virtually queuing up to paint him. He was immortalised in a poem by Lord Byron and figurines were also made of him.

After retiring from the ring Cribb went on to run a pub in London.

Sir Stafford Cripps

(1889—1952)

For the whole of his parliamentary career Sir Stafford Cripps was a Labour Member of Parliament for Bristol East. Before joining the Labour Party he was carving himself a career in the legal profession and qualified as a barrister specialising in patent and compensation cases.

A year after joining the party in 1929, he was appointed Solicitor-General, a post which at the time brought with it a knighthood.

However, as Sir Stafford Cripps was not yet an MP he stood for parliament in a by-election in 1931 in Bristol East, a Labour stronghold. He was elected and represented the constituency for nineteen years until he stood down because of poor health. He was succeeded by Tony Benn.

Although Sir Stafford was often in conflict with his party he held various important government posts. He was probably best known as the austere post-war Chancellor of the Exchequer and Minister of Economic Affairs.

He died in Switzerland, where he was convalescing, two years after retiring from politics.

Adge Cutler
(1930—74)

Local singer Alan John Cutler was better known as Adge Cutler, the original lead vocalist for the Scrumpy and Western Folk Group, The Wurzels.

Adge was a prolific writer of simple folk songs about the people and districts of Bristol, farming, cider and Somerset villages. His songs won fans from all over the West Country and in 1966 Adge and his band were signed up by EMI records and released their first album, which was recorded in a pub.

The Wurzels were on the verge of national fame when *Drink Up Thy Zider* entered the charts, just missing out on the Top 40, coming in at number 45. However, the record sold more than 100,000 copies. National television and radio appearances followed and the song went on to become the 'national anthem' of North Somerset and is now the theme song for Bristol City Football Club.

Tragically, just as it seemed Adge Cutler would achieve the fame and fortune his songwriting skills demanded, his life was cut short when he was killed in a car accident near Chepstow on 5th May 1974. He was driving home from a concert in Hereford when his car left the road near the Severn Bridge and overturned.

The rest of the band decided to stay in show business without him and are still going strong.

Sir Humphry Davy

(1778—1829)

Cornishman Humphrey Davy intended to study medicine but changed his mind when meeting Dr Thomas Beddoes who was on a geological expedition in Cornwall.

Dr Beddoes asked Davy to be superintendent of his grandly named Pnuematic Institution which he opened at Hotwells in Bristol. Davy immersed himself in the work at the laboratory in Dowry Square preparing gases to treat illnesses.

In 1799 he discovered the anaesthetic properties of nitrous oxide or laughing gas. Davy used this as both a painkiller and a recreational drug with his new found friends the poets Samuel Taylor Coleridge and Robert Southey. Nitrous oxide has long been used as as anaesthetic before surgery.

In the same year Davy published his West Country Collections and Researches containing his first scientific essays.

While he was working at the Institution Davy lived with Dr Beddoes at Rodney Place, Clifton. He left Bristol for London and the newly established Royal Institution where, at the age of twenty-five, he was made Professor of Chemistry. He was awarded a knighthood by the Prince Regent in 1812 for his impact on 19th century science.

Sir Humphry Davy is best known for his invention of the safety lamp which was to save the lives of thousands of miners. He suffered a stroke while in Rome and died in Geneva on his way back to England.

Paul Dirac

(1902—84)

At a commemoration service in Westminster Abbey Paul Dirac was described by Stephen Hawking as 'probably the greatest British theoretical physicist since Newton'. In his oration Professor Hawking went on: 'He has done more than anyone this century, with the exception of Einstein, to advance physics and change our picture of the universe'. Yet the name of Paul Dirac is hardly known, even in his native city.

He was born in Bishopston, one of three children whose father was a Swiss-born teacher. On leaving the old Merchant Venturers' School he studied electrical engineering at Bristol University, graduating with first class honours. Dirac then transferred to the mathematics department where again he gained first class honours.

After leaving university he went to Cambridge University as a graduate student. Dirac was a pioneer of quantum mechanics, producing his PhD thesis in 1926 on the subject. He predicted the existence of the dual particle of the electron, the positron, leading to a whole new world of antimatter. Positron emission therapy is now much used in medicine.

In 1933 he shared the Nobel Prize for Physics 'for the discovery of new and productive forms of atomic theory' with an Austrian scientist.

For nearly forty years Dirac held Cambridge's prestigious Lucasian chair of mathematics, following in the footsteps of Isaac Newton. After retiring from the university he moved to America and became Professor of Physics at Florida State University.

He is commemorated in Bristol by a modern sculpture of two coloured concentric cones made of cement and glass fibre standing on the Harbourside.

William Chatterton Dix

(1862—1898)

William Dix was a prolific hymn writer who wrote many of his verses during bouts of poor health.

He produced several volumes of hymns, one of which he entitled *St Raphael's Hymns* after the church on Cumberland Road where he was a chorister. The church, which overlooked the Floating Harbour, was destroyed by German bombs during a night-time air raid on Bristol in the Second World War.

Dix was the son of a surgeon and writer, who gave him his middle name in honour of the Bristol boy poet Thomas Chatterton, about whom he had written a biography. After leaving Bristol Grammar School Dix worked for an insurance firm, eventually becoming a manager. He died in the Somerset village of Cheddar where he was buried in the parish churchyard.

Some of Dix's best known hymns include *What Child Is This?*, *Joy Fills Our Inmost Hearts This Day* and *Alleluia! Sing to Jesus*! He also wrote the popular Epiphany hymn *As With Gladness Men of Old* while he was confined to his sickbed.

Harry Dolman

(1897—1977)

Harry Dolman was a giant of both Bristol's industrial and sporting life. By trade he was an engineering designer who took over the firm he worked for, Brecknell Dolman and Rogers at Easton. It dated back to 1860 and specialised in making food packing machinery and coin-operated machines such as parking meters.

Harry Dolman made the headlines when at the age of sixty-three he married his secretary, Marina, who was nearly four decades his junior.

He became chairman of Bristol City Football Club in 1949, a post he held for some thirty years. He designed the first set of floodlights installed at City's ground in the early 1950s.

Since her husband's death in 1977, Marina Dolman has been president of Bristol City and is a regular supporter at matches. One of the club's stands is named after Harry Dolman.

Eliza Walker Dunbar

(1845—1925)

A year after qualifying as a doctor Eliza Walker Dunbar was appointed Resident Medical Officer at the hospital for Women and Children, then on St Michael's Hill. However, after a year she left because of the hostility of some of the male staff.

At the time medicine was very much a preserve for men; medical schools were not accepting women, even though Eliza, the daughter of a surgeon, had qualified for her medical degree at the University of Zurich in 1872.

After leaving the children's hospital Dr Dunbar was appointed the first Honorary Medical Attendant at the Read Dispensary for Women and Children in Hotwells. She later set up a private hospital for women and children, the Walker Dunbar Hospital in Clifton Down Road. The building is now being converted into residential accommodation.

Dr Dunbar lived in Oakfield Road, Clifton, where a plaque commemorating her pioneering work was unveiled by Dr Beryl Corner.

Jo Durie
(1961—)

As a child Jo Durie lived within almost a ball's throw of the tennis courts at Redland which may have helped her to decide on a career.

She put Bristol on the tennis map in 1984 when she was Britain's great white hope at Wimbledon when she was twenty-three. She was then rated world number five and reached the quarter finals.

But unfortunately Jo never won the title in the next ten years of her professional career. She retired from Wimbledon in 1995 with a knee injury.

Jo, who went to Clifton High School, has since worked as a television commentator and a tennis coach.

During her playing career, she won two Grand Slam mixed doubles titles, and was ranked the No.1 British player for most of her career. She won the British national singles titles six times & the national doubles title eight times.

Jo also won two tour titles in 1983 at Mahwah New Jersey and Sydney, and in the same year also reached the semi-finals of the US Open and the French Open.

Maria Edgeworth

(1767—1849)

Novelist Maria Edgeworth lived most of her life in Ireland helping her father to manage his estate, but the family spent two years in Clifton from 1791. Their home was in Princes Buildings, near the Suspension Bridge.

During their time in Clifton the Edgeworth's became friendly with Dr Thomas Beddoes, who married Maria's sister.

Although many of her books were about the Irish people and peasant life in Ireland she also wrote books on education, as well as witty and improving stories for children. Some of her stories were set in Bristol.

Maria Edgeworth's best known adult novel was *Castle Rackrent*, the fictional memoirs of an Irish servant.

Amelia Edwards
(1831—1892)

Amelia Edwards, who lived for almost thirty years in Westbury-on-Trym, shares with Rajah Rohumman Roy the distinction of having one of the most unusual tombs in the city. Her grave in St Mary's Churchyard, Henbury, is marked with an Egyptian style memorial reflecting her fascination with that country.

She was the daughter of an army officer and is best remembered as an egyptologist, although she also worked as a journalist for magazines and newspapers, penned Christmas stories, novels and books about her travels. One of her publications, *A Thousand Miles up the Nile*, featured her own hand-drawn illustrations.

Amelia Edwards took much interest in ancient Egyptian culture and was concerned about the destruction of the antiquities that was going on in that country. She co-founded the Egyptian Exploration Fund with the aim of researching and saving ancient Egypt for posterity.

In her will she bequeathed most of her Egyptian Library to University College, London and also left funds for the founding of the United Kingdom's first university Chair of Egyptology.

Elizabeth I and Elizabeth II

(1533—1603 and 1926—)

When Queen Elizabeth I spent a week in Bristol in 1574 she was given the red carpet treatment and a purse containing one hundred pounds in gold.

Lavish entertainment was laid on to amuse the monarch including an elaborate water pageant with mock battles between ships.

The Queen is reputed to have described St Mary Redcliffe Church as 'the fairest, goodliest, and most famous parish church in England'. However, the source of this remark has never been discovered. Rather curiously, there is no documentary evidence — not even a single line in the church records to support this remark.

Nevertheless Elizabeth I is regarded with much veneration in Redcliffe for she gave back some of the endowments, mainly land, seized by her father and brother. She also gave the church permission to set up a free grammar and writing school in the parish, the forerunner of the present St Mary Redcliffe and Temple School.

Elizabeth I is remembered in the church by a colourful life-size wooden effigy standing on a stone plinth near the north porch.

When one of her successors, Elizabeth II, made her first official visit to Bristol as monarch in 1956 she was given a private tour of the church. On a second visit in 1995 the Queen and the Duke of Edinburgh joined nearly 1,000 charity and voluntary workers in a special service.

As the Queen signed the visitors' book the Rev Tony Whatmough asked if she remembered her first visit. Her Majesty told him that St Mary Redcliffe was not the kind of church that one forgot.

Princess Eugenie

(1826—1920)

Eugenie Montijo, later to become Empress of France, and her sister Paca, later Duchess of Alba, lived in Clifton in the 1830s. These daughters of a Spanish nobleman arrived from their family home in Paris to attend a boarding school run at numbers 1–3 Royal York Crescent by a Mrs Rogers.

Of her time at Clifton — just three months from April 1837 — the young Eugenie is reported as saying:

> *Do not think there are any public amusements here. Everyone stays at home and one never sees a fashionable man in the street.*

However, she returned for a couple of days in 1889 booking into St Vincent's Rocks Hotel, now a block of flats, near the Clifton Suspension Bridge.

Eugenie went back to Paris and met Louis Napoleon who was to become Emperor of France. The couple married in 1853.

Her old school closed in 1855 and the building has since been converted into flats, but is now known as Eugenie House.

Keith Floyd

(1943—2009)

Keith Floyd was arguably the first celebrity chef on television. True, Philip Harben was the first chef on the small screen but his presentation was rather formal, whereas Keith Floyd became known for his flamboyant style and eccentric character.

Always wearing a bow tie, taking a tipple or two of wine whilst preparing and cooking a meal, working without a script and barking orders at the cameraman who was filming him, Keith Floyd gained a nationwide audience.

He was so popular that from the 1980s onwards he made twenty-six series of television programmes ranging from six to twelve episodes. One series was filmed in India.

Keith Floyd's broadcasting career started after he published his first book, *Floyd's Food* in 1981. This led to a ten-minute chat show about recipes on the old *Radio West*, an independent station based in Bristol.

By the age of twenty-eight he was running three restaurants in the Clifton and Redland areas of Bristol: Floyd's Bistro in Princess Victoria Street, Floyd's Restaurant in Alma Vale Road and Floyd's Chop House in Chandos Road. One of his customers was a television producer who asked him if he could cook on television. The rest, as they say, is history.

Keith Floyd wrote more than thirty books about cookery as well as several autobiographies, and owned gastro-pubs. Explaining his financial downfall he admitted that whilst he enjoyed cooking he was no businessman.

He spent his childhood in Wiveliscombe, Somerset, and was educated at the local public school, Wellington.

Before making a career in the kitchen, Keith Floyd had various employments. These included a stint at the *Bristol Evening Post* with some accounts claiming that he was a cub reporter and others that he was an assistant to the editor. There was also a spell in the 3rd Royal Tank Regiment.

Keith Floyd, who married four times, was so well-known that when he died of a heart attack most of the national newspapers published lengthy obituaries. A plaque commemorating his life can be found on the exterior wall of his first bistro.

Dr Edward Fox

(1761—1835)

Edward Fox has gone down in medical history as a pioneer of the promotion of humane methods in the treatment of mental illness. Instead of the straightjacket he ordered as little restraint as possible and introduced occupational therapy.

He is credited with opening the first purpose-built private mental asylum for the insane at Brislington House, on the southeast outskirts of Bristol in 1804. Here Dr Fox catered for the rich, providing accommodation for their servants and stabling for coaches. Brislington House was designed as a group of detached houses, which were later joined together.

In his treatment programme he experimented with hypnotism and promoted the healthy benefits of sea-bathing, building Knightstone Baths at Weston-super-Mare for the use of his patients. Brislington House was run by the Fox family for around 150 years.

Dr Fox was a physician at the Bristol Royal Infirmary for twenty years from 1857 and a Lecturer in the Bristol Medical School from 1869-1874. He was called in to give advice when George III was reported to be mad.

Sir Francis Freeling

(1764—1836)

Francis Freeling was no politician, statesman or wartime hero, yet on his death the daily business of the House of Lords was stopped so that tributes could be paid to him. He was the son of a sugar baker, born on Redcliffe Hill, who put his stamp on Britain's postal service.

After leaving Colston's School Freeling started work as an apprentice in the Bristol Post Office. It wasn't long before his 'talents, rectitude of conduct and assiduity in his duties' were quickly recognised by his managers.

At the age of twenty he was transferred to Bath where he worked as protégé to John Palmer, Comptroller General, and inventor of mail coaches. A couple of years later he was working at the General Post Office in London where he was promoted to the role of surveyor. He was later made principal and resident surveyor, joint secretary and eventually sole secretary of the Post Office. This prestigious post was held by Freeling for thirty-eight years until his death.

A baronetcy was conferred on him in 1928 in recognition of more than half a century of public service to the country.

When he died, the Duke of Wellington told the House of Lords:

The Post Office under his management has been better administered than any Post Office in Europe or in any part of the world.

Freeling is remembered by a rather grand marble tablet in St Mary Redcliffe church and in the name of a block of flats nearby. An inscription on the tablet records that:

…by employment of great talents and by unblemished integrity grounded upon Christian principles he acquired and returned the favours of three successive sovereigns.

Professor Richard Gregory

(1923—2010)

Richard Gregory was Professor of Neuropsychology, and Director of the Brain and Perception Laboratory at the Medical School, Bristol University. However, he was best known amongst thousands of school children from all over the country as the founder of The Exploratory Hands On Science Centre in the city. It opened at the Victoria Rooms and later moved to Brunel's Old Station, Temple Meads.

This was the first such science exploratory in Britain showing through various exhibits the relationship of science, nature and art to life. By the time it closed in 1999 it had attracted more than two million paying visitors. It evolved into Explore @Bristol which received lottery money from the Millennium Fund that was used to build a new centre.

Professor Gregory had a long and distinguished career as a scholar. He was interested in the way humans perceive the world and was a man on a mission to get more children interested in science.

He was the son of an astronomer and first director of the University of London Observatory. After graduating from Cambridge University he lectured there, and in 1976 was appointed Professor of Bionics at Edinburgh University. Four years later he moved to Bristol where he spent the rest of his life.

After retiring from his Personal Chair at Bristol University in 1988 Richard Gregory became Emeritus Professor and moved from the medical school to the Department of Psychology.

He took part in hundreds of radio and television programmes discussing science and was a 'castaway' on the BBC's *Desert Island Discs* programme.

Despite retirement he was still busy writing books and accepted Visiting Professorships at several American universities. In recognition of his work nine British universities awarded him honorary degrees.

Amongst his recreations Professor Gregory, who lived in Clifton, listed punning and pondering.

William Friese-Greene

(1855—1921)

William Friese-Greene is claimed by some to be the English inventor of cinematography after he shot some film in London's Hyde Park.

His interest in photography started when he was a youth. After leaving Queen Elizabeth's Hospital he was apprenticed to photographer Maurice Guttenberg, who had a studio in Queen's Road, Clifton. Later Friese-Greene set up on his own studios which he called the Photographic Institute.

There he built a camera with a single lens to record real movement as it happened. Friese-Greene took it to London's Hyde Park where he shot twenty feet of families walking, open-top buses and hansom cabs. This made him the first person to create moving pictures on screen, however cinematography purists say that he did not create perforated strips of film.

Making the camera bankrupted Friese-Greene and he sold the rights to the patent. It was one of seventy-eight patents he had taken out for developments ranging from photographic cigarette cards to airships and x-rays.

Friese-Greene, who was born William Green in College Street near College Green, later married Swiss Helena Friese, taking on her name and adding an 'e' to his own. He died in London while attending a conference and was buried in Highgate Cemetery where his tomb was designed by Sir Edward Lutyens. The emerging photographic industry held Friese-Greene in so much respect that at the time of his funeral cinemas across the country observed a two minute silence.

Christopher Fry

(1907—2005)

During the 1940s and 1950s Bristol-born Christopher Fry was regarded as one of the country's leading playwrights with his work being produced on both sides of the Atlantic. Some of the best known actors of the day including Richard Burton and Laurence Olivier took on leading roles in his plays.

He was born Christopher Harris, the son of a builder who gave up the trade to become an Anglican lay reader. The young Harris eventually took the name Fry from his maternal grandmother.

Fry started work as a teacher but later turned to acting and was appointed director of the Tunbridge Wells Repertory Theatre. He started to write after serving in the Second World War and becoming well known for such works as *A Phoenix Too Frequent* and *The Lady's Not For Burning* which he wrote in 1947. The title was to be parodied by Prime Minister Margaret Thatcher in a speech in 1980 when she suggested that the 'lady was not for turning'.

Joseph Fry

(1728—1787)

Mention the name Fry and many people would immediately think of chocolate. But Joseph Fry, founder of the JS Fry and Sons chocolate firm, was something of an entrepreneur. He also set up a printing and typesetting company with a printer, William Pine, and had interests in several other business ventures, among them a pottery and a soap making firm.

Joseph Fry was born into a Quaker family in Sutton Benger, Wiltshire. He went into business in Bristol as an apothecary in Small Street but started making chocolate in the 1750s. A few years later he took over the business and patented chocolate recipes of the late Walter Churchman, another local apothecary.

As the business expanded Joseph Fry set up a factory on nearby Union Street, which with its tall red brick chimneys dominated the Pithay area for 150 years. In the 1920s the firm moved to a purpose-built factory on a 228-acre green field site at Keynsham, midway between Bristol and Bath. Its name, Somerdale, was chosen in a national competition.

One of Fry's most popular products was its Five Boys Milk Chocolate bar. Its wrapper depicted a boy going through various moods, from sorrow to joy, as he ate the chocolate.

When Joseph Fry died the business was managed initially by his widow Anna and later his son Joseph Storrs Fry. The Fry family gave some of their wealth to Bristol University, hospitals and other good causes in the city.

The firm stayed in the family until it eventually merged with another Quaker chocolate maker, Cadbury, in 1919. Eventually the Fry name disappeared. In 2010, following the takeover of Cadbury Plc by Kraft Foods, the closure of the Keynsham site was confirmed to take place in 2011.

Rev Canon Percy Gay

Not many clergymen could claim the popularity that surrounded Canon Percy Gay. For forty-five years he was vicar of St George's Church, Brandon Hill, and was so liked that twenty-two organisations across the city enlisted him as their padre. He was looking after everyone from actors to seafarers, and was also in big demand as an after dinner speaker.

Canon Gay's church was threatened with closure by the Bishop of Bristol in 1966. The poor structural condition of the building made it unsafe and it seemed that the cost of repairs to a sagging roof and bulging wall was prohibitive.

But Canon Gay was not a man easily deterred by crumbling fabric. He prepared a restoration scheme and appealed to Bristolians for £5,000 for emergency repairs. Their generosity was such that three times that amount poured in and six months later St George's reopened for services.

The death of Canon Gay coincided with a dwindling congregation. Many of the nearby houses were being converted into offices and the church never flourished again. It was finally declared redundant as a place of worship in 1984.

But a new use for the church was on the horizon when St George's Music Trust was formed to turn it into a music centre. The building's acoustics have helped it to become one of Britain's loveliest chamber concert halls. Performances by some of the world's greatest musicians are often broadcast from St George's by the BBC.

Eric Gill

(1882—1940)

It's probably little known that a fascia board of a shop in Bristol was one of the first places where a typeface that was to become popular all over the world was seen.

This was in 1929 and the typeface was Gill Sans, designed by the sculptor, calligrapher and writer Eric Gill. He used it for the name board of a bookshop owned by his friend, bookseller and publisher Douglas Cleverdon (one of the books produced by Cleverdon was of Gill's artwork, all printed from the original blocks).

Unfortunately, this piece of typographic history was lost when the shop on the corner of Charlotte Street and Park Street was bombed during the Bristol Blitzes of the Second World War.

However, some of Gill's sculptures can still be seen including Prospero and Ariel at the BBC's headquarters in London and the Stations of The Cross in Westminster Abbey. Locally, some of his inscriptions can be seen on monuments in the village church at Mells near Frome.

Gill started his working life as an apprentice to an architect but became fascinated by the world of print, and went to evening classes to learn about typography. He designed numerous typefaces, many of which are still used, but was famous for Gill Sans which became the letter of the railways, appearing on their timetables, signs, and engine plates.

Edward Godwin

(1883—1886)

Although he contributed to Bristol life in so many ways Edward William Godwin is hardly, if at all, remembered today. Born in Old Market Street and later living in Portland square, he was an architect, running his own practice by the age of twenty-two, a designer of furniture, textiles, wallpaper and tiles. He was also an antiquarian, interior decorator, stage and costume designer and newspaper theatre critic.

One of his major architectural projects was the restoration of St Mary Redcliffe church between 1843 and 1872. Some of the work was paid for by Alderman Thomas Proctor who asked Godwin to design a gentleman's mansion — now the Lord Mayor's Mansion House — for him on the edge of Clifton Down.

Other examples of Godwin's work includes the ornate drinking fountain near the Mansion House; the village hall at Westbury-on-Trym; houses at Rockleaze, Sneyd Park, and Perry's Carriage Works in Stokes Croft.

Soon after the *Western Daily Press* began publication Godwin was writing theatre reviews for the newspaper. This gave him the opportunity of meeting the actress Ellen Terry who was performing at the Theatre Royal. Godwin, who designed her costumes, ran away with the young actress. During their relationship which lasted about six years, Ellen Terry bore him two children.

He later died in London after setting up an architectural practice there, the furniture of which he designed himself.

WG Grace

(1848—1915)

Dr William Gilbert Grace, or 'WG' as he was better known, is best remembered for his cricketing skills rather than the use of the stethoscope. He was regarded as the champion and the greatest player the game has ever produced.

He was born into a cricketing family at Downend and his first recorded public match was against Bedminster Cricket Club when he was nine years old. Six years later he was playing for a Bristol side against an all-England XI on the Downs.

WG qualified as a doctor in 1879 after studying at Bristol Medical School and St Bartholomew's hospital, London. He had a surgery on Stapleton Road for fifteen years, often getting a locum to stand in for him so he could play his beloved cricket. He was still dedicated to his profession however; when eight men were killed in an explosion at Easton Collliery in 1886 Dr Grace arrived to tend the injured.

Almost as soon as he joined Gloucestershire County Cricket Club in 1864 WG was selected to play for the Gentlemen Players match. He went on to captain the county side, and played for England on twenty-two occasions and captained the team for two test matches against Australia. During his career he made 126 centuries, scored 54,896 runs and took nearly 3,000 wickets.

But WG wasn't the only cricketer in his family; his daughter Bessie was selected for the first XI at Clifton High School. In one match, watched by her father, she scored 28 runs, taking three wickets and one catch. In another match she took ten wickets.

WG Grace retired from medicine and moved to London in 1898 although another ten years were to pass before he played his final game of first class cricket.

Cary Grant
(1904—1986)

Archibald Leach, who was born in Horfield and went to the local Fairfield Grammar School, was better known as Hollywood heart throb Cary Grant.

His interest in the theatre and show business was kindled as a youngster by a visit to Bristol Hippodrome. It was there that he later got a job as a lighting assistant before going to the United States in 1920 with a troupe of acrobats, and started his Hollywood career in the 1930s. His screen debut came in *This Is The Night*.

Cary Grant was known as a suave and debonair screen lover and comic actor and was one of the best known stars of his generation. He appeared with some of the great screen names of the day, among them Marlene Dietrich, Ingmar Bergman, Audrey Hepburn, Mae West and Deborah Kerr.

Grant's film classics include *North By Northwest*, *To Catch a Thief* and *The Philidelphia Story*.

He retired from show business in 1966, and received a special Academy Award for his 'unique mastery of the art of screen acting'.

Despite his fame and fortune Cary Grant never severed his links with Bristol, bringing all four of his wives to his native city. He frequently visited his mother in a nursing home in Clifton. It was not unknown of him to let the local newspapers know that he was back in town.

A bronze statue of Cary Grant holding a film script stands in Millennium Square. He is also commemorated by a plaque at his birthplace.

Francis Greenway

(1777—1837)

There can't be many criminals who have had their portrait on a bank note. But it happened to an architect from Bristol who narrowly escaped the gallows.

Francis Greenway was born in Mangotsfield, brought up in Ashton and worked in Clifton where he designed the Clifton Hotel and Assembly Rooms. This imposing building in The Mall is now the home of the Clifton Club.

Greenway started work on the project when he was twenty-nine but never saw the job completed. For when the hotel and assembly rooms opened their doors with a grand ball, the architect was languishing in the city's Newgate Prison (the Mall Galleries are now on the site). He had been sentenced to hang for forging a promissory note for £250 in connection with work on a house in Clifton.

However, Greenway won a reprieve and the judge's original sentence was commuted to transportation for fourteen years.

When he arrived in Australia in 1813 it seems that Greenway wasted no time in letting the great and the good know that he was an architect. Commission then followed commission as he was asked to design some of Sydney's main public buildings, among them the Parliament Building, the law courts and many churches. His work so impressed the Governor of Sydney that he appointed him Civil Architect.

By now Greenway had become regarded as a 'son' of Australia and to honour his skills his portrait was put on some of the country's ten dollar bills. He died in Australia aged sixty having never returned to Bristol.

A plaque commemorating Greenway was unveiled at the entrance to the Clifton Club on the 200th anniversary of his birth by the Australian High Commissioner.

Sarah Guppy

(1770—1852)

Inventor Sarah Guppy was taking out patents throughout most of her life, the last one when she was aged seventy-four.

Her ideas included improvements for a suspension bridge, predating the work of Isambard Kingdom Brunel by nearly twenty years.

A woman of much vision, Sarah Guppy came up with a method of keeping ships free of barnacles, and produced designs for a four poster bed with built-in exercise equipment. There was also the multi-purpose tea and coffee urn that could cook eggs and keep toast warm. Her final patent concerned a method of making ships waterproof.

Sarah Guppy lived in Queen Square before moving to Richmond Hill, Clifton, where a plaque on her home commemorates her life. Her son Thomas was a skilled engineer who both funded Isambard Brunel and collaborated with him on some of his projects.

Eddie Hapgood

(1908—1973)

Edris Albert Hapgood, better known as Eddie, who was one of football's greatest full backs, turned down a contract to play for Bristol Rovers because it meant giving up his job as a milkman, and delivering coal in the summer months instead.

Rovers' management must have rued the day that they insisted Hapgood would have to take on the close-season job they were offering. Within a year he was playing for Arsenal's first team at the start of the club's glory days in the 1930s. Altogether he made 434 appearances for the club.

As well as captaining the side up to the outbreak of the Second World War, Hapgood became the regular captain of England. He made his England debut against Italy in Rome when he was twenty-four. The match ended in a 1–1 draw. Altogether he was capped thirty times. Hapgood also played in some of the most famous matches of the century including the 6–3 defeat of Germany in 1938.

After his retirement as a player in 1945 he moved into football management, firstly with Blackburn Rovers, then with Waterford and later there was a six year stint with Bath City.

Eddie Hapgood was born in the Dings area of St Philips. It was while playing for his local club, St Philips Adult Juniors in the Downs League, that a director of Bristol Rovers spotted his talent and offered Hapgood a first team place at £8 a week.

John Hare

(1752 —1839)

At the age of twenty-one years John Hare made his way from the village of Crowcombe on the Quantocks into Bristol hoping to make his fortune. Arriving on the outskirts of the city he couldn't find anywhere to rest so spent the night in an orchard sleeping under the stars. The next day Hare vowed that should he become a wealthy merchant he would build a chapel on the land which had become his makeshift bed.

He found premises near Queen Square where he experimented with different ways of making seamless oil floorcloth. The business took off and with an expanding order book Hare moved to a bigger factory at Temple Gate.

Fifty-six years later his dream of building a chapel came to fruition. He bought the land where he had slept and built Zion Congregational Church beside Bedminster Bridge. It opened in 1830 and was big enough to hold one thousand worshippers.

Hare lived for another ten years to see his church fully established. He was buried in the chapel, near the pulpit, but his remains were later re-interred at Arnos Vale Cemetery.

Zion church closed in the 1980s because of a dwindling congregation but John Hare's building still stands and is now used as offices.

Minnie Haskins

(1875—1957)

At the end of his Christmas Day radio broadcast in 1939 King George VI quoted from a poem called *God Knows* written by a grocer's daughter from Warmley. The writer, Minnie Haskins, was unaware the King was going to recite from her poetry and neither did she hear the broadcast.

The poem was included in an anthology that Minnie Haskins published in 1908.

It's said that inspiration for the verses came to Minnie at her home in Warmley. At the time she was standing at a balcony window looking down a lamplit pathway to the garden gate. Her poem begins with the words: 'I said to the man who stood at the Gate of the Year.'

Minnie Haskins was a student at the London School of Economics and later lectured there on social sciences.

She was invited back to Warmley during the Festival of Britain Celebrations in 1951 to unveil a plaque on her former home which had been turned into offices. It is now a residential and nursing home.

The Hawkins family

Herbert Hawkins was a newspaperman who founded the *Bristol Evening Post* in 1932 after a newspaper war in the city with Lord Rothermere. Herbert's father was editor of the *Bristol Times and Mirror*, which was taken over by the *Western Daily Press*, which in turn was taken over by Herbert's son Walter.

Bristolians did not take lightly to the introduction of the *Bristol Evening World* in 1929 owned by Lord Rothermere, owner of the *Daily Mail*. They wanted their local news brought to them by a locally owned paper. Bristolians raised enough money to set up a new paper with all the company's directors living in the city.

The first edition of the *Bristol Evening Post* hit the streets on 18th April 1932. Herbert Hawkins was the paper's first managing director until his death in July 1941. Since the first day the paper has always carried the legend: 'The paper all Bristol asked for and helped to create'.

Herbert Hawkins was succeeded by his son Walter who served in the post until 1967 and was also chairman from 1960–74.

Further down the Hawkins Family generations was Richard, editor of the paper from 1960—1964. He became editor at the age of thirty and at the time was the youngest editor of any evening paper in the country.

Ruby Helder

(1890—1938)

Although she became an international operatic singer Emma Jane Holder is hardly remembered today.

She was born in the Glasshouse pub in Easton where her father was the landlord. As a youngster Emma often entertained the regulars with her singing and was encouraged to take formal lessons. On finding that someone else in her class had the same surname, Emma Holder adopted the stage name of Ruby Helder.

Her deep and powerful singing voice astonished everyone who heard her perform. Her aunt, housekeeper to the great Scottish music hall star Harry Lauder, made arrangements for her to train at the prestigious Guildhall School of Music in London. She later received tuition from one of the outstanding figures in British music, Charles Santley.

Ruby made her operatic debut at the Queen's Hall, London, and before long she was awarded recording contracts, and invited to sing at concert halls around the world.

Enrico Caruso, the renowned Italian opera singer, reckoned Ruby's range of two octaves was only two notes short of his own. He introduced her to the Metropolitan Opera House, in New York, and the American audiences took her to their hearts.

She also sang in Philadelphia and Chicago, wooing those who came to hear her with a repertoire that included *Come into the Garden, Maud; Good Night Beloved;* and *Be Thou Faithful Then You'll Remember Me*.

Ruby Helder returned to England in 1920 with an American architect and artist Chelsey Bonestell whom she married that summer at Marylebone Register Office.

After making an extensive tour of Italy the couple settled in America where Ruby died in a hotel at Hollywood at the age of forty-eight.

Sarah Ann Henley

(1863—1948)

The story of Sarah Henley is one that outstrips fiction. It's a tale that seems too good to be true but one that really happened. This young woman had a remarkable escape from instant death after jumping from the Clifton Suspension Bridge in an apparent suicide attempt.

Twenty-two year-old Miss Henley from Easton made her way to the bridge after a lover's tiff. However, she was blown by the wind across the Bristol side and then turned a complete somersault so that she was now falling feet first to the ground 250 feet below.

The wind blew under Miss Henley's wide skirt and her clothes acted like a parachute, gently slowing down the rate of her fall. It seems that this saved her life. It took the police more than an hour to carry Miss Henley on a stretcher to the infirmary where she was treated for shock and severe internal injuries.

Sarah Henley recovered from her experience and later married. She went on to live until she was eighty-five and was buried in Avon View Cemetery.

Her fall from the bridge on 8th May 1885 is part of its history, with Miss Henley being the first person to survive a drop during the twenty years in which it had then been open and a temptation to suicide.

William Herapath

(1797—1868)

William Herapath, born in a public house, started his working life by following in his father's footsteps as a maltster and running the Pack Horse on Lawrence Hill. However, Herapath, who had shown an interest in chemistry since his early teens, went on to become a pioneer of toxicology.

He was one of the founders of the Chemicals Society of London and lectured on chemistry and toxicology at the Bristol Medical School which he had helped to set up. Within two years of the school opening in 1826 Herapath was appointed its Professor of Chemistry and Toxicology, a post he held until his death.

As a forensic expert he gave evidence in the murder trial of Mary Ann Burdock. He discovered arsenic in the stomach of her victim fourteen months after her burial. Herapath's examination of the exhumed body was instrumental in Burdock being taken to the gallows. From then on Herapath was frequently asked to make chemical analyses in cases of poisoning which came before the courts. They were often *causes célèbres* bringing Herapath a certain amount of public fame.

As well as chemistry he was vice president of the Bristol Political Union and when the Municipal Reform Act became law in 1835 he was elected to the Bristol council as a Liberal.

Damien Hirst

(1965—)

Known as the 'bad boy' of Britart, Damien Hirst, the son of a car salesman, was born in Bristol but grew up in Leeds and went on to Goldsmith's College, London.

He has continually challenged the boundaries between art, science, the media and popular culture — in 1995 he won the Turner Prize for his provocative work.

One of his installations involved displaying sections of sliced cows in large tanks of formaldehyde. On another occasion he exhibited a platinum cast of a human skull encrusted with diamonds. He has also opened a restaurant in London's Notting Hill called The Pharmacy which has its walls lined with medicine cabinets and drinks with medicinal names.

Damien Hirst has exhibited in art galleries and museums around the world including Australia, Korea, America and many European countries. His works fetch large sums whenever they are put up for sale.

He has also developed an interest in pop music designing covers for pop band albums and the set for *Glastonbury*, a play about the annual music festival in Somerset.

According to the *Sunday Times* 2010 Rich List Damien Hirst has a personal wealth valued at £215 million. He now lives in Devon, working from his home there and studios in London.

Bruce Hockin

(1936—)

This popular television presenter talked himself into the record books in August 1988 as the longest-serving news presenter on television in this country.

Bruce Hockin progressed from local newspapers to TV and wasn't at all convinced in the early days that he would make it as an anchorman. However, he became the most readily recognised face on television in the West Country.

His television career started with HTV's predecessor Television Wales and West (TWW) as a researcher and then as an on-screen reporter. He became regular presenter of HTV's evening news as he says, 'out of the blue' one day in August 1968 and stayed in front of the camera for three decades.

Bruce Hockin presented 125 hours of live television every year as well as documentaries. Everyone from Prime Ministers to the Rolling Stones have been among his interviewees.

In the course of his job he has walked the high wire, rode a unicycle and had knives thrown at him!

Bruce Hockin was born at Exmouth, educated at Bude and Bideford Grammar Schools and went on to serve an apprenticeship in journalism with the *Bideford and North Devon Gazette*. Later he joined the *Western Mail* in Cardiff, working in a number of journalistic roles.

He now lives in retirement with his wife Caroline in the house that they have lived in for more than thirty years.

Professor Dorothy Hodgkin

(1910—1994)

This eminent scientist became Bristol University's first woman chancellor in 1971. She held the office for seventeen years during which time she was also President of the International Union of Crystallography and a member of the USSR Academy of Science.

At the time she was the only non royal woman to hold the post of chancellor in a British university. Not content with just the ceremonial aspect of the role, Professor Hodgkin spent much time involved with the welfare of students.

Professor Hodgkin, the eldest of four daughters, took an interest in science when she was a child, having set up a small laboratory in her bedroom. She went on to read chemistry at Somerville College, Oxford, a subject not normally studied then by women. After graduating she started doctoral studies at Cambridge.

Professor Hodgkin spent much of her time working with penicillin and insulin for which she received many awards. She was awarded the Noble Prize for Chemistry in 1965.

Bristol University has named one of its buildings after her.

Charles Holden

(1875—1960)

Perhaps because it has been there for more than a century we tend to take it for granted, but Bristol's central library on College Green is something of a treasure. Not just for the wealth of information inside but as an architectural and historical charm.

The library was designed and completed by Charles Holden, then an unknown architect who was twenty-seven years old. It was the subject of a competition and Charles Holden entered it under his boss's name.

With its marble staircase leading from the entrance hall to the first floor Holden's library won national acclaim for its design.

It was later described by Sir Nikolaus Pevsner, the art historian and architectural scholar as 'Holden's most remarkable work'.

Charles Holden's design includes the frieze which decorates the Deanery Road exterior of the library. The twenty-one figures cast in stone are the work of Bristol-born sculptor Charles Pibworth. Among them are seven saints with literary connections including Augustine, Cuthbert and the Venerable Bede.

Charles Holden designed many buildings both in Britain and abroad. From 1931 onwards he designed twenty or so of London's underground stations.

Samuel Jackson

(1794—1869)

Samuel Jackson was a watercolour artist who never moved from Bristol, living for a while in Canynge Square, Clifton, and also in Freeland Place, Hotwells, which he included in one of his works.

He was one of the group of amateur and professional artists known as the Bristol School and mainly painted landscapes.

Samuel Jackson's range of subject matter was wide ranging from romantic scenes of Sea Mills and Henbury valley, to views of city streets.

He was a friend of Isambard Brunel and was commissioned to paint the construction of his Clifton Suspension Bridge. This went on show at the city's oldest club for businessmen, The Commercial Rooms, so that the public could understand the general effect of the bridge's design on the Avon Gorge.

John James CBE

(1907—1996)

John James, a docker's son born in the bleak back streets of Bedminster, was regarded as Bristol's greatest modern benefactor and one of the country's most successful post-war businessmen.

He opened his first radio shop in 1946 on the strength of his Royal Air Force gratuity of one hundred pounds and within a year had ten branches. It was during his time in the RAF before and during the Second World War that John James learnt about wireless as a radio operator.

By 1958 he owned the world's largest radio and television chain with 300 stores which he sold for £6 million. However, John James had no intention of retiring from the business world and instead started a chain of furniture stores which he sold in 1979 for £25 million.

The death of his third daughter Dawn in a 1963 road accident (when she was just twenty-one), devastated him so much that he set up a £10 million charitable trust in her memory. Through the trust Dawn's share of the family's wealth could be directed to charity centred on Bristol. The trust was later merged with the John James Foundation which focuses on supporting education, health services and the elderly. One of the biggest gifts was one million pounds for a brain scanner at Frenchay Hospital.

John James also financially helped to start Windmill Hill City Farm which is on the site of his childhood home. By way of thanks farm managers said they would give Mr James a cabbage once a year grown on the spot where his house had stood.

William Jessop

(1745—1814)

William Jessop was an engineer who started working on canal construction when he was sixteen years old. His work all over the country put him into the first rank of leading civil engineers.

He was commissioned to build Bristol's Floating Harbour and the New Cut so that there would be a permanent high tide in the docks. This was essential if the port was to expand, take bigger ships and provide a quicker turn round for them with the unloading of their cargoes. Bristol's prosperity was threatened as traders began to choose others ports to avoid the harbour's 10 metre tides.

Jessop's scheme was completed in 1809 with the River Avon being re-directed into the New Cut, giving the City Docks a commercial future. The new waterway was also used for navigation, with early passenger steam packets sailing to south Wales and Ireland from a jetty by the Louisiana pub, formerly the Bathurst Hotel.

It had taken more than a thousand English and Irish labourers five years to dig out the New Cut and install lock gates. Their main tools were shovels, picks and wheelbarrows and gunpowder was used to blast through the rock.

Jessop appointed his son to supervise this mammoth task which cost £600,000, three times the budget figure. The workmen celebrated the completion of the project with a hog roast accompanied by lots of ale!

Pero Jones

(1753—1798)

One of the bridges across the Floating Harbour in the centre of Bristol is named after Pero Jones, a 'house boy' for a wealthy merchant family in the city.

He was born on the island of Nevis in the West Indies and bought as a slave by a sugar planter and merchant John Pinney. Pero was bought, along with his two sisters, for £115.

Pero Jones was Pinney's slave in the West Indies for nearly twenty years and was then brought to England with his master's family in 1783. They eventually settled in a fine house which Pinney had built in Great George Street. Today it is a museum known as the Georgian House.

Pero, who was a respected servant, died when he was forty-five years old.

In March 1999 a horned footbridge built across the Floating Harbour at Narrow Quay was named after Pero and commemorates all those who were enslaved by Bristol's merchants and planters.

Sir Allen Lane

(1902—1970)

Penguin Books was the brainchild of Bristol-born Sir Allen Lane, who conceived the idea on his way back to London from a meeting in Devon with the crime writer Agatha Christie.

As he waited for his train at Exeter station, Lane could only find popular magazines and reprints of Victorian novels available on the bookstall. He immediately recognised the need for good quality contemporary fiction at an attractive price. Lane was also determined that his new range of books should be available not only in traditional bookshops but also on railway platforms and in High Street chain stores.

He was born in Cotham, the eldest of three sons, and went to Bristol Grammar School. He joined the publishing house of Bodley Head in 1919 as an apprentice to the founder and his relative John Lane. The young Lane worked his way up through the ranks and left the firm as Managing Director to set up Penguin.

The first Penguin books appeared in 1935 costing just sixpence and were a selection of novels, crime writing and biography by contemporary authors including Agatha Christie, Ernest Hemingway and Eric Linklater. Within a year three million Penguin paperbacks were sold.

In 1960 Allen Lane fought a literary *cause célèbre* in the Old Bailey with Penguin's publication of the unexpurgated version of DH Lawrence's *Lady Chatterley's Lover*. He was prosecuted under the obscenity laws but the charges were dismissed. More than 200,000 copies of the book were sold.

In the 1960s Allen Lane took Penguin Books public, became a millionaire, and was knighted.

Stephen Lansdown

(1958—)

Not content with co-running a multi-million pound financial business at the time, avid football fan Stephen Lansdown became chairman of his beloved Bristol City Football Club in 2003.

He has been following the club's fortunes for 20 years, serving on the board of directors for about half that time. In March 2011 Stephen Lansdown announced that he would stand down as the club's chairman at the end of the season. He told a press conference at the City Ground that it "was time he took a fresh approach" to his involvement with the club. Although he will no longer be a board member Mr Lansdown said his ties with the club "were unbreakable" and that he would remain a shareholder and Bristol City's "biggest benefactor".

Stephen Lansdown, the only son of a carpenter, has his roots firmly entrenched in the Bristol area. He was born at Almondsbury and educated at Thornbury Grammar School.

He started the stockbroking business of Hargreaves and Lansdown with Peter Hargreaves in one room in 1981, equipped with only a typewriter and a second-hand desk. Since then the company has grown to employ more than 650 people who look after the affairs of some 350,000 clients. In 2009 the firm moved from offices in Clifton to a new £30 million building on Bristol's harbourside.

In the same year Stephen Lansdown sold a stake of 4.7% in the business for a reported sum of £47.2 million, which he put towards the cost of building Bristol City's proposed new football stadium at Ashton Vale.

According to *The Sunday Times* Rich List of 2010 Stephen Lansdown has a private wealth of £452 million. He is now a non-executive director of the firm and has moved from Bristol to Guernsey.

Despite the heady world of high finance, with its interest rates, spreadsheets and board meetings, Stephen Lansdown says he still loves to hear the roar of the crowd at Ashton Gate.

He has described the scheme for a new 30,000-seater stadium at Ashton Vale, costing around £80 million, as a "once-in-a-lifetime opportunity for the club, the city of Bristol and the Southwest". His big ambition, he says, is to see his beloved Bristol City promoted to the Premiership.

John Latimer
(1824—1904)

It's often said that no one recorded the history of Bristol more faithfully than John Latimer in his Annals of Bristol. Yet, remarkably, he was not a Bristolian.

Latimer was born in Newcastle and at the age of twelve started keeping a diary recording local events in Northumberland. He became a journalist on Tyneside, arriving in Bristol when he was aged thirty-four. Latimer was appointed editor of the *Bristol Mercury*, a post he held for a quarter of a century.

But he is best known for his three-volume annals which covered Bristol's history from the 16th century to 1900. Each volume runs to around 700 pages and Latimer has recorded events in the city chronologically. He noted everything from debates at city council meetings, often including remarks made by councillors, to the progress of work on Brunel's Clifton Suspension Bridge and his Great Western Railway, and the deaths of eminent citizens.

Nothing, it seemed, escaped Latimer's eyes as he fastidiously trawled through such documents as council records and old newspapers, He even recorded some of the most minor cases heard by the local courts.

Latimer loved Bristol so much that he settled in the city until his death. He is buried in Bristol Cathedral.

Sir Thomas Lawrence

(1769—1830)

As a boy Thomas Lawrence had a precocious talent for sketching and painting customers at his father's pub. By the age of twelve he had his own studio and was later considered pre-eminent amongst portrait painters of his time.

Lawrence was born in Redcross Street, Old Market, and went to school at Cotham. His father was an innkeeper who ran the White Lion pub in Broad Street, now the site of the Grand Thistle Hotel. He later moved to the Bear Hotel in the Market Place at Devizes.

Such was the standard of Lawrence's work that he was appointed 'Painter in Ordinary' to King George III. After being knighted in 1815 he travelled around Europe painting political and military leaders.

By the time he became president of the Royal Academy five years later famous celebrities, including the actress Sarah Siddons, were virtually queuing at Lawrence's studio for a sitting.

His funeral service took place at St Paul's Cathedral and was a national event with sixty-four carriages in the procession. A bust of Lawrence carved by another local person, Edward Hodges Baily, is in Bristol Art Gallery.

Vincent Stuckey Lean

(1820 —1899)

The Central Library at College Green didn't cost Bristol's ratepayers a penny thanks to the generosity of Vincent Lean. Lean, who died at the age of seventy-nine, was a barrister who had devoted his life to the arts, literature, natural history and travel. This public spirited citizen left £50,000 for the library to be built.

In his will Vincent Lean said he was making the bequest:

> *… for the further development of the free libraries of the city, and with special reference to the formation and sustentation of a general reference library.*

He also bequeathed his collection of about 5,000 books to the library. It was opened in 1906 replacing the library in King Street which had been running since 1613 and counted amongst its borrowers the poets Coleridge and Southey.

Richard Long

(1945—)

Taking a walk in the countryside has brought fame and fortune to the Bristol-born artist and sculptor Richard Long. He uses the landscape as his material, marking places out with sculptures. It could be something as simple as a circle of stones, trenches or even the footprints he has left behind.

These he removes or recreates as exhibits, sometimes with actual materials, or as drawings, maps or photographs.

Richard Long, who trained at the Royal West of England Academy of Art in Bristol for three years in the 1960s, has been in involved in more than 300 group or solo exhibitions. His diary of shows resembles a gazetteer with events from Australia to Tokyo. He became Bristol's first Turner Prize winner in 1989.

Many museums have Richard Long's work on display and his *Delabole Slate Circle*, acquired from the Tate Modern in 1997, is in Bristol's Museum and Art Gallery.

A permanent installation is on view in the main lobby of Hearst Tower in New York City entitled *Riverlines*. It's the biggest wall work Long has ever made, measuring about 35 x 50 feet (11 x 15 metres).

Sir Bernard Lovell
(1913—)

As a schoolboy Bernard Lovell had set his mind on working in the radio business and playing cricket. But that changed after a teacher took him to a public lecture at Bristol University called 'The Electric Spark'. It turned out to be a decisive moment for Bernard Lovell. Shortly after his eighteenth birthday he enrolled as a student at the university to read physics — the start of his journey to becoming a celebrated astronomer and scientist.

Bernard Lovell was born at Oldland Common near Bristol and went to the local Kingswood Secondary School, which is now named after him. After graduating from university in 1934 he went on to do research for two years before moving to Manchester University where he was appointed Assistant Lecturer in Physics.

During the war Bernard Lovell worked for the Air Ministry and was awarded the Order of the British Empire for his research into the use of radar for detection and navigation purposes. In 1951 he became Professor of Radio Astronomy at Manchester University.

He was the creative force behind the funding, construction and use of the 250-foot-diameter radio telescope at Jodrell Bank Exploratory Station, Cheshire. It was completed in 1957 in time to thrill the world with its tracking of the first Russian Sputnik space satellite.

Sir Bernard was one of the first western academics allowed to view secret Russian special installations. In recognition of his contribution to science he was honoured with a knighthood in 1961.

Gary Mabbutt MBE

(1961—)

For Gary Mabbutt it was a case of following in his father's footsteps. Ray Mabbutt had played football for various clubs including Bristol Rovers. In 1978 Gary signed with Rovers as an apprentice and turned professional a year later.

He was diagnosed by the club doctor as having diabetes but Gary Mabbutt did not let the illness hamper his career. Indeed, he became something of an iconic figure for many children who suffered from the condition.

On one occasion he appeared on the BBC's Children's programme *Blue Peter* where he demonstrated injecting insulin into an orange to show how he dealt with diabetes on a daily basis.

Gary Mabbutt signed for the First Division club Tottenham Hotspur in 1982 and played for the side for sixteen years. During this time he turned out for Spurs 618 times and captained the club in the FA Cup finals of 1987 and 1991.

He retired from football in 1998, not because of diabetes but because his left knee was fragmented.

Gary Mabbutt was awarded the MBE in 1994 for services to football. He promotes the work of the charity Diabetes UK, appearing in various television programmes to highlight the condition.

Emma Marshall

(1828—1899)

Novelist Emma Marshall is worth a story herself. Although she had been writing for many years she became extremely prolific after her husband's bank in Corn Street crashed with liabilities of around £3 million. She worked hard to support her husband — he had not only lost his job but also faced big debts — herself and their nine children.

More than two hundred stories flowed from Emma Marshall's pen. The first, *Happy Days at Fernbank,* was about the moral education of two little girls and was published in 1861. From then onwards she turned out romances, historical novels, children's books and short stories and wrote for a range of publications from women's magazines to religious papers.

Some of her novels were set in Bristol. One of them, *Bristol Diamonds*, was subtitled *A story about the Hot Wells in the year 1773*. Another was a historical romance based on the life of the philanthropist Edward Colston.

Emma Marshall was born in Norwich into a banking family, arrived in Bristol when she was nineteen and lived in Victoria Square, Clifton. She married bank worker Hugh Marshall who was the son of the vicar of nearby Christ Church.

His job took the family around the country but they eventually settled in Leigh Woods, where Emma died. She was buried in the churchyard at Long Ashton. When her husband died he was buried beside her.

John Loudon McAdam

(1756—1836)

The man who gave his name to a revolutionary system of road building that turned rough tracks into smooth surfaces lived in Bristol at the peak of his fame.

John McAdam, the inventor of macadamised roads (now generally known as tarmac) was a Scotsman by birth who in 1816 was appointed Surveyor of the Bristol Turnpike Trust, being responsible for 146 miles of roads. Unsurprisingly, Bristol's roads were among the first to benefit from the new surface. He instructed that stones should be graded and laid in three levels, with the smallest stones crushed and laid as a top surface. These roads were said to be 'macadamised'. Later, tar was laid over the top of the crushed stones, giving an even more durable surface known as tarmacadam. McAdam's experiments left him impoverished. He asked Bristol Corporation (City Council) for financial help but this was rejected. McAdam then petitioned the House of Commons which, five years later, voted him a grant of £2,000.

He was later appointed Surveyor General of Metropolitan Roads for Great Britain.

He lived in Berkeley Square from 1805 to 1808 and from 1815 lived at Sion Hill. A plaque commemorating him was affixed to the house in Berkeley Square by a later resident.

McAdam was the first president of the Commercial Rooms, a club in Corn where businessmen could discuss affairs of the day and carry out deals. The club is now defunct but the premises have been turned into a pub called The Commercial Rooms.

Precious McKenzie MBE

(1936—)

This diminutive weightlifter — just 4 foot 11 inches tall — won four Commonwealth Games gold medals in a row and came fifth in the Munich Olympics. He was also world bantam-weight champion five times.

McKenzie, who was nicknamed the 'Pocket Rocket', came to Bristol, where he was hugely popular, to escape apartheid in South Africa. He settled in Southville but now lives in New Zealand. While in Bristol he trained at the Empire Gym in St Paul's.

Various sources report that the Queen was late for an official engagement because she was so determined to see the weightlifter win his third Commonwealth gold medal. He was awarded the MBE in 1974.

George McWatters

(1922—2006)

Businessman George McWatters was the last family member to sit on the board of John Harvey and Sons, the wine merchant which took the name of Bristol Cream sherry around the world.

He was the great grandson of the founder John Harvey and joined the firm in 1947 after army service in the Second World War. Mr McWatters became chairman in 1956 but resigned ten years later after the firm, which had been in his family for 174 years, was taken over by Showerings Limited, maker of the Babycham drink.

Mr McWatters went on to become chairman of a footwear firm, and the independent television broadcaster HTV, and a director of other companies. He also served on the board of many charitable organisations.

His great grandfather, the son of a sea captain, is said to have given up a maritime career because he suffered from seasickness. He joined a wine merchant in Denmark Street as an apprentice, eventually taking over the business. Its trade was based mainly on Spanish and Portuguese wines including port and sherry.

One of Harvey's sherry blends became known as Bristol Cream after being described as such by a customer. The term 'Bristol Milk' first became well-known in the 17th century as the name of a sherry or sweet wine from Jerez in Spain. Harvey's publicity material says the earliest reference to this can be found in a manuscript from a traveller's diary dated August 1634. It reads: "And so, with a cup of Bristol Milk, we parted with our honest and grave host, and bade this sweet city adieu."

Harvey's prospered under the founder's two sons, John and Edward. The latter was succeeded in 1910 as chairman by his nephew John George Harvey who died in 1919. His brother Eddy took over the business, and in 1939 he was followed as chairman by John St Clair Harvey.

The firm became famous in more than a hundred countries for its sherry, in particular Bristol Cream.

John Miles MBE

(1940—)

It's often been said that the only way to succeed in many walks of life is by moving to London as that's where it all happens, especially in the heady world of show business.

But Bristol-born John Miles has turned that hoary old tale on its head. In 1958 he started managing pop groups from his parents' home in Clifton Wood. By 1963 he was handling more than 450 groups, with about 40 of them permanently working in clubs in Germany.

Three years later he decided to concentrate on just a few acts. The first person to walk into his office was Adge Cutler, who with the Wurzels became internationally known for his so-called Scrumpy and Western style. Adge wrote and sang songs about manure, cider, Somerset villages and Bristol suburbs.

John Miles' business has grown over the years with him becoming one of the country's leading and most respected showbiz managers. He now looks after 16 television presenters including Carol Vorderman, Noel Edmonds, Des O'Connor, Nick Knowles and Timmy Mallett. He has represented some of them for more than thirty years. "I look after everything they do, whether they write books, make DVDs, television and radio shows or personal appearances," John explains.

His entrepreneurial flair came to the front when he became ringmaster of *BBC Radio 1*'s travelling pop show which was watched by thousands of holidaymakers on beaches around the country and heard by millions more on radio. The programme ran from the 1970s into the 1990s.

John Miles built the *Radio 1 Road Show*'s travelling stage, equipped with some of the most sophisticated electronic wizardry to put the programme on air every summer weekday. It was driven from seaside town to seaside town by his brother Tony, who quickly became known on air as Smiley Miley. BBC Enterprises also gave the brothers a licence to sell merchandise, from car sun visors to sticks of rock bearing the *Radio One* logo. He still runs his business from home, although he's crossed the River Avon to live in the secluded Gordano Valley in North Somerset.

John Miles helps to raise millions of pounds to help cancer sufferers through his chairmanship, for the last 17 years, of the Friends of Bristol Oncology Centre. He heads the prostate cancer care and research centre appeal at Southmead Hospital and is chairman of the Gloria Miles Cancer Foundation as well as being involved with stem cell research at Hammersmith Hospital, London. In recognition of his services to charity he was awarded the MBE in 2009.

Hannah More

(1745—1833)

Born at Fishponds in Bristol, Hannah More was an evangelist, religious writer, playwright, anti-slavery campaigner and social reformer who cared passionately about the less well-off. One of five daughters of a schoolmaster, she taught at the Academy for Young Ladies in Park Street which was run by her elder sisters.

Miss More was keen to establish herself as a playwright and moved to London in the 1770s, mixing with people from the theatrical world. She was friendly with the actor David Garrick but after his death became increasingly drawn to the world of evangelical Christians and started writing her own moral works.

Having settled with her sisters at Barley Wood, just outside Wrington in the Mendip Hills, Hannah More became concerned about the poorly paid miners and farmers and their families in the surrounding villages. She set up a chain of village schools with the first one in Cheddar, and offered educational, spiritual and financial help.

Hannah More spent her final years in Clifton where she died at the age of eighty-eight leaving some £30,000, which she had made from her writings, for religious societies and charitable institutions.

Samuel Morley

(1809—1886)

Every year that he was Member of Parliament for Bristol, businessman Samuel Morley gave £20,000 to the city for local good causes. He was Liberal MP for the city between 1868 and 1885.

Shortly after he died a bronze statue of him was unveiled near Bristol Bridge before thousands of spectators. The statue has been on the move several times and currently stands on the edge of the Broadmead shopping centre. There is also a memorial to Morley in Bristol Cathedral.

Morley, who came from the north of England, was the son of a hosier. His wealth came from extending his father's business with mills in several north country towns.

Johnny Morris

(1916—99)

For twenty-one years farm manager Johnny Morris became a national television celebrity thanks to his gift of mimicking the sounds of animals and putting words in their mouths.

He was the main presenter of the *Animal Magic* programme, which was produced from the BBC's Bristol studios. It was aimed at educating children about animals but the audience was boosted by a large number of adults as well. *Animal Magic* became the first big hit television show featuring animals.

Wearing a zookeeper's uniform Johnny wandered around Bristol Zoo where he was filmed having 'conversations' with the animals. Sometimes animals were taken into the studios. The programme ran for 454 editions starting in April 1962.

Before *Animal Magic* took to the airwaves Johnny Morris was already known as a television storyteller in the guise of the 'Hot Chestnut Man'. He appeared on the small screen roasting chestnuts in a brazier and telling his young audience stories.

His broadcasting career started in radio with a series called *Pass The Salt* in which he tried other peoples' jobs. A series of travel programmes which were produced in Bristol followed. *Johnny's Jaunts* not only took the presenter and his microphone around England but to various countries including Germany, Turkey, South America and the South Seas.

Johnny Morris was 'discovered' by a BBC executive who heard him entertaining regulars at his local pub with his storytelling.

When he died he was buried with his wife in the garden of their home in Berkshire. National newspapers reported that he was buried wearing his trademark zookeeper's hat.

B.1805
D.1898

George Müller
Founder of the ASHLEY DOWN ORPHANAGE, BRISTOL

Westfield
Production

George Muller, founder of orphanages.

George Muller

(1805—1898)

George Muller, the son of a Prussian tax collector, was a German pastor who arrived in Bristol in 1832 and became one of the city's greatest social reformers. One of his first initiatives was to establish the first Brethren Assembly in the city at Great George Street, where the congregation at one time numbered a few hundred.

Six years later he set up his first orphanage in some rented terraced houses in Wilson Street, St Paul's. There was room for twenty-six children but the need was so great that George Muller eventually built five large homes on Ashley Down which accommodated a total 2,050 children at any one time.

Not once did Muller ask for money but instead believed in the power of prayer to supply his needs and those of the children in his homes. His prayers were answered for he received £1.5 million in donations. This helped him care for more than 10,000 children who otherwise would have been destitute.

Muller died at his orphanage and the whole of Bristol stopped for his funeral. Many firms gave staff the day off and newspapers reported that several thousand people packed the streets near Arnos Vale Cemetery to pay their last respects as the funeral cortege passed.

The first Muller orphanages in St Paul's have long been demolished but the buildings on Ashley Down, bordering on Gloucestershire County Cricket Club's headquarters ground, still stand. But they closed as children's homes in the 1950s and have been put to other uses.

William James Muller

(1812—1845)

W J Muller from the Bristol School of artists won fame nationally for his watercolour landscapes and his painted scenes from his travels around the world.

He was born on Hillsbridge Parade – it was near the site of the Bath Road bridge — the son of a Prussian refugee who was the first curator of what was to become Bristol City Art Gallery. From the age of fifteen he was apprenticed to James Baker Pyne, a follower of Turner, for two years.

Muller became known for his scenes of the Avon Gorge, the Reform Riots in Queen Square in 1831 and the burning of the Bishop's Palace. Three years later he was travelling around Europe, especially Venice and later to Egypt and Lycia in modern Turkey and Egypt.

Muller returned to Bristol in 1845 for health reasons where he died. Towards the end of the 19th century, Muller was considered one of the greatest painters of the English landscape. Some of his works are in Bristol Museum and Art Gallery, and there is a memorial bust of him in Bristol Cathedral.

Sir Henry Newbolt

(1862—1938)

The poet Sir Henry Newbolt was inspired by his old school to write some of his most famous lines. Newbolt arrived at Clifton College as a dayboy when he was fourteen, rising to become Head Boy. From Clifton he won a scholarship to Corpus Christi College, Oxford, where he read classics.

He pursued a career in law as a barrister but later turned to writing poetry, stories for boys, novels and a naval history. In all he wrote twenty-eight books and published twelve volumes of poetry.

His first volume, *Admirals All*, sold 21,000 copies in a few months. The collection included some of the most quoted lines from English poetry, most notably these from his poem *Vitaï Lampada*:

> *There's a breathless hush in the Close tonight —*
> *Ten to make and the match to win —*

and:

> *Play up! play up! and play the game!*

The 'Close' to which Newbolt referred was the field at Clifton College on which numerous cricket matches have been played.

Newbolt was knighted in 1915 and made a Companion of Honour in 1922.

Nipper
(1884—1895)

High up on the wall of an office building on the corner of Park Row and Woodland Road, leading into Clifton, is a dog carved in stone. This is Nipper the dog that appeared on labels of His Master's Voice (HMV) records.

Nipper was born in Bristol in 1884 and was so named because of his tendency to nip the backs of visitors' legs. His owner was Mark Barraud (1848–1887), a scenic artist at the Princes Theatre nearby which was destroyed during one of the many wartime blitzes on Bristol.

When Mr Barraud died his younger brother Francis gave Nipper a home and painted him listening to the family phonograph. The painting was sold to the newly formed Gramophone Company for £100.

Nipper died in 1895 but he lived on as the famous trademark for His Master's Voice labels for nearly a century. His image was also used on everything from the firm's needle boxes to promotional novelties.

Sir George Oatley

(1863—1950)

No Bristolian can imagine the city without its majestic Wills Memorial Building, towering 215 feet over the city centre from its lofty position at the top of Park Street.

This mock-Gothic tower, the centrepiece of Bristol University's campus, was designed by Sir George Oatley, a tanner's son, who became one of the West Country's foremost architects and shaped much of the present face of Bristol.

Apparently, his design for the Wills Memorial Building was inspired by a dream in which he saw a tower on a hill with shields all around it. Once he got down to his drawing board Oatley took just three weeks to come up with the full plans — and that was working nights only.

Oatley's tower incorporates around fifty rooms including a library and council chamber as well as the magnificent Great Hall. This is used for major events at the university including its degree ceremonies. At the top of the tower Oatley built an octagonal belfry which houses Bristol's largest bell, Great George.

The Wills Memorial Building cost just over half a million pounds — well over the original budget of a hundred thousand – and was officially opened in 1925 by King George.

Amongst Oatley's other commissions were St Monica's Home of Rest on the downs, the Homoepathic Hospital at the top of St Michael's Hill and St Edyth's Church at Sea Mills.

In 1912 he was appointed architect to St Mary Redcliffe church and looked after this magnificent building until his death. He was responsible for the church's great restoration of 1930–1933, and designed the vaulted undercroft which he built beneath the dramatic flight of steps leading to the North Porch.

Patrick O'Brien

(1760—1806)

Patrick O'Brien's height caused something of a sensation as he walked the streets of Bristol for he was 8 foot 4 inches tall. For almost a quarter of a century he put himself on show as a freak at fairs all over the country making so much money that he was able to retire at the age of forty-four.

He then settled in his lodgings at Hotwells spending much time socialising in his local alehouse. The landlord had a special mahogany chair made for him, the seat being twenty-seven inches wide and specially strengthened to take O'Brien's weight of fifteen stone. It was sold in 1979 for £2,000.

One newspaper reported that O'Brien would lean out of the first floor window at his home and kiss women as they passed by! It was also said that he would light his pipe by lifting the lid off the oil lamps which then lit the streets.

Even at his funeral O'Brien was still attracting the crowds. Newspapers reported that some 2,000 people packed the roads leading to the graveyard in Trenchard Street, off the city centre. No funeral hearse could be found that was large enough to carry his coffin so it had to be carried to the grave by fourteen men working in relays.

Many years after his death builders digging foundations for a new school accidentally discovered his coffin. A surgeon was given permission to exhume the body and examine it for academic purposes before it was reinterred.

Nick Park CBE

(1958—)

Who would have thought that two plasticine characters eighteen centimetres high would capture the affections of international audiences and some much-coveted awards in the entertainment industry?

Wallace and Gromit, the main characters in a series of animated films, are the brainchild of Nick Park of Aardman Animations of Bristol.

Wallace, an absent-minded inventor, is a cheese enthusiast while his faithful canine sidekick Gromit appears to be more intelligent than his master. The former is voiced by the actor Peter Sallis while Gromit remains silent and communicates through facial expressions and body language. The BBC has described the characters as 'some of the best known and best loved stars to come out of the UK'.

Nick Park's creativeness has made him and his team fairly wealthy as well as putting Bristol on the animation map.

He had started making a film called *A Grand Day Out*, featuring Wallace and Gromit, while a student at the National Film and Television School. It was finished shortly after he joined Aardman in 1985 to work in their studios with Peter Lord and David Sproxton. The film won a BAFTA award.

Three of the plasticine duo's short films — *A Grand Day Out, The Wrong Trousers* and *A Close Shave* — have been seen by audiences in nearly 50 countries. Their first feature film, *The Curse of the Were-Rabbit*, won an Oscar for Best Animated Feature Film of the Year among many other awards.

They have also starred in a six-part BBC television series – *Wallace and Gromit's World of Inventions* – in which they examined their favourite inventions from around the world.

The couple, with a little help from Nick Park, have also teamed up with a number of major companies to advertise their products in television commercials. In Japan they help to sell insurance policies whilst back home they can be seen on the small screen endorsing tea, cars and an electricity supplier.

Nick Park was awarded the CBE in 1997 and received an Honorary Doctorate from the Royal Academy of Art in 2006.

William Patterson

(1795—1869)

William Patterson was born in poverty in Scotland and by the age of fifteen was living in London where he was apprenticed to a shipbuilder.

He later moved to Bristol where he found work in a shipyard at Wapping Wharf. When its owner was declared bankrupt Patterson and his son took over the business.

Patterson's lasting claim to fame was his construction of Isambard Kingdom Brunel's Atlantic paddle steamer the *Great Western*. He also built the hull of the *SS Great Britain*. Probably as a result of his connection with Brunel, Patterson's order book expanded with warships, brigantines, racing yachts and steamers being built at his yard.

Unfortunately, disaster struck in 1851 when a wooden-hulled paddle steamship, *The Demerara*, ran aground just outside the entrance locks at Cumberland Basin. She was being towed by a tug from Patterson's yard bound for the River Clyde to have her engines fitted. The canny Scot was undeterred, ordering his men to remove the *Demerara*'s paddles so that she could be repaired and converted into a passenger sailing ship. She was then given the name *British Empire*.

During the Crimean War Patterson lost some £20,000 on orders from the Royal Navy and he was forced to sell his assets.

William Patterson retired to Liverpool, where he died. His son stayed in Bristol, specialising in salvage work.

The Paty Family

This family of builders, architects and masons has been described as 'the makers of 18th century Bristol'. They were the foremost designers and craftsmen of their time in the city.

The Patys were responsible for making Clifton a flagship of Georgian splendour with its imposing squares, crescents and terraces. They also created wonderful facades and interiors for private and public buildings.

It was a large family but the main players were Thomas Paty (1713—1789) and William Paty (1758—1800). Thomas, the eldest son of the statuary mason James, was an architect and craftsman. Amongst other works he was responsible for laying out many streets and for the rebuilding of both Bristol Bridge and St Nicholas Church as well as for dressed masonry and carving on the Exchange in Corn Street, Clifton Hill House and Royal Fort House.

William Paty's best known works are a merchant's house in Great George Street, now the Georgian House museum, Blaise Castle House and Christ Church in the centre of the city.

Robert Pearsall

(1795—1856)

Robert Pearsall, who had a talent for composing music from an early age, was born on Clifton Hill but when he was seven his family moved to the first of two addresses in Kingsdown. They later bought Willsbridge House at Bitton, in South Gloucestershire.

Pearsall studied at Lincolns Inn to be a lawyer and after being called to the bar in 1821 set up his barrister's chambers in Small Street, close to Bristol's law courts. But after four years he gave up all thoughts of a career in the legal profession to devote the rest of his life to music and moved to Germany.

His love of music dated back to childhood days. When he was just thirteen years old Pearsall wrote a cantata, *Saul and the Witch of Endor* which was printed privately.

He was a founder member of the Bristol Madrigal Society (later Bristol Chamber Choir) and wrote almost two-dozen madrigals for the group including one with a title reflecting his local background: *Oh Who Will o'er the Downs So Free*.

Pearsall is probably best remembered for his arrangement of *In Dulci Jubilo*, sung at Christmas by the choir at King's College, Cambridge.

Although he spent the second half of his life in Germany, Pearsall returned to his home city on many occasions.

Admiral Sir William Penn

(1621—1670)

Contemporary writers described Admiral Sir William Penn as the most distinguished Bristolian of the 17th century. Penn, who was born in the Redcliffe area of the city was addicted from his youth to maritime affairs and had a dynamic naval career.

This second son of a merchant and sea captain entered the Navy as a boy and was a captain when he was twenty-one years old. It wasn't long before he was made Rear Admiral of Ireland, becoming Vice Admiral the following year. Penn was later made Vice Admiral of England, and a General in the first Dutch War which ended with a failed expedition against the Spanish West Indies.

In the Second Dutch War Penn was promoted to Great Captain Commander of the Fleet under James, Duke of York. He was made Governor of Jamaica when the island was captured.

Penn, who was knighted by Henry Cromwell, died in Essex but left instructions that he should be buried in St Mary Redcliffe church, not far from his birthplace. It was also the church where his parents were married.

His armour, along with an elaborate marble memorial stone, is displayed high up on the south wall of the church tower.

When Penn died the King owed him money so he rewarded his son William (1644—1718) with nearly 50,000 acres of land in North America, where he established a Quaker colony.

Many people sailed from Bristol with the younger Penn who had chosen the name 'Sylvania' for the colony but the King insisted on prefacing it with 'Penn' as an honour to his father. Pennsylvania is the only state in America which bears or incorporates the name of its founder.

Rev. Dr John Percival

(1834—1918)

The Reverend Dr John Percival was the first headmaster of Clifton College which opened in September 1862. On the first morning he preached to sixty-nine boys who were on the register for the opening term.

He was only twenty-eight years old when he was appointed to Clifton but had worked under Dr Arnold of Rugby School, although for only two years. He set out to build at Clifton a school that would be 'brave, gentlemanly, Christian and classically educated'.

John Percival was also instrumental in setting up Clifton High School in 1877 and played a major role in early discussions to have a university in the city. He published a pamphlet calling upon the 'great towns' to set up 'intellectual centres' like Oxford and Cambridge. Percival visualised provincial towns providing the buildings and equipment whilst the established universities would supply the lecturers.

He stayed at Clifton College for seventeen years, leaving to become President of Trinity College, Oxford, and then returning to Rugby as its headmaster. He was later appointed Bishop of Hereford.

At his own request John Percival was buried in Clifton College Chapel although he could have been interred in Hereford Cathedral.

John Pinney

(1740—1818)

This was a merchant who made his wealth through his inherited sugar plantations in the Caribbean islands of St Kitts and Nevis. With his friend James Tobin he set up his own sugar company. The couple also owned ships and loaned money to plantation owners and took over both the plantations and slaves of those who could not pay their debts.

Pinney's business made him a wealthy man enabling him to have a grand house built for himself and his family in Great George Street, off Park Street. John Pinney brought with him to Bristol a slave as his personal assistant. He purchased Pero Jones when the boy was just twelve years old.

When he died Pinney left a fortune of £340,000. His son, Charles, was Mayor in 1831 at the time of the Bristol Riots over the Reform bill.

Since 1939 his home has been open to the public as the Georgian House museum, an example of an 18th century merchant's house.

Samuel Plimsoll MP

(1824—1898)

Countless lives have been saved at sea thanks to the work of Samuel Plimsoll. His long campaign for better conditions for seafarers led to him being called the 'Sailor's Friend'.

Plimsoll was born in Colston Parade, Redcliffe, and went on to have a varied career started his working life as a solicitor's clerk in Bristol. He later managed a brewery, became secretary of the Great Exhibition of 1851 at Crystal Palace and a coal merchant in London, before eventually being elected as Member of Parliament for Derby in 1868.

He spent much time campaigning for the improvement of conditions on ships, especially those that were overloaded. Being born on the edge of the Bristol dockside he would have been aware of the vessels that foundered because of having too much cargo on board, some of them before even leaving the port.

Plimsoll's determination led to the passing in parliament of the Merchant Shipping Act of 1876, which gave the Board of Trade power to detain unsafe or overloaded ships. It also ordered every ship owner to mark a maximum loading line on the side of their vessel. This was known as the Plimsoll Line and was adopted by ships all over the world.

Memorials to Plimsoll can be found in almost every port in the world and Bristol is no exception. High up on the wall of his birthplace is a plaque commemorating him. A bust of Plimsoll stands on Capricorn Quay, part of Bristol's historic floating harbour. One of the swing bridges on the Cumberland Basin flyover is also named after him.

George Pocock

(1796—?)

A 'thrashing machine' for chastising errant schoolchildren was one of the inventions of teacher, Methodist preacher, chapel organist and father of eleven, George Pocock. It's not known though whether he used it at the grandly named Prospect Place Academy in Kingsdown, where he taught.

It was Pocock's abiding interest in aviation that thrust him into the public spotlight. News of his invention of a horseless carriage powered by kites — he called it a Charvolant — even reached the papers in Chicago. Pocock had found a way of using two kites on a single line to provide enough power to draw along a buggy carrying several passengers.

On one occasion sixteen members of his family travelled from Bristol to London by this new form of transport. For this particular journey four Charvolants were used travelling at around twenty miles an hour. One of them is said to have overtaken a mail coach.

Pocock caused something of a sensation when he put his daughter, Martha, in a wicker chair and hoisted her up into the air using kites. Fortunately, she came to no harm and went on to become the mother of cricketing legend W G Grace.

Despite demonstrating the Charvolant before George IV at Ascot and taking it many hundreds of miles around the country, Pocock's invention never caught on.

Undeterred, in 1827 he published a book entitled *The Aeropleustic Art or Navigation in the Air by the use of Kites, or Buoyant Sails*.

Martin Pring

(1580—1626)

Martin Pring was given Sir Walter Raleigh's permission for a trading and exploration expedition that discovered Cape Cod, North America. He set out from the port of Bristol at the age of twenty-three with two ships under his command, the flagship *Speedwell* and the *Discoverer*, financially backed by some of Bristol's wealthiest merchants.

His voyage of 1603 reached Massachusetts Bay which was renamed Whitson Bay after the Bristol merchant and benefactor John Whitson. The name was changed again seventeen years later when the Pilgrim Fathers landed there and called it Plymouth Harbour.

Pring is credited with exploring and mapping the islands, harbours and rivers of New England. His ships returned to Bristol loaded with sassafras, a plant used in medicines.

He was later employed by the Dutch East India Company who put him in command of a fleet of five vessels sailing to the East Indies, eventually rising to become the company's Commander of Naval Forces.

A memorial tablet to Pring can be found in St Stephen's Church where he was buried.

Thomas Proctor

(1812 —1876)

It's not everyone that builds a home, or to be precise a mansion, and gives it away. However, that is just what Alderman Thomas Proctor did.

He commissioned local architects George and William Godwin to design the house on one of the most prestigious sites in Clifton. Two years and £2,500 later Alderman Proctor was able to move into Elmdale House on the corner of Canynge Road and The Promenade. The Godwins had built him a three-storey, twenty-two room gentleman's residence with a spacious drawing room, billiards room, and galleries.

Proctor lived at Elmdale House for about seven years until 1874 when he announced his intention to give the house to Bristol Corporation (now City Council) on his wedding anniversary. His gift came complete with fixtures, fittings and furnishings as well as a £500 cheque to help cover the cost of any repairs or decorations.

The house became the official residence of the Mayor and Mayoress during their term of office, a role it plays to this day, and was renamed The Mansion House.

Such generosity was typical of Alderman Proctor whose wealth came mainly from his chemical, manure and fertiliser business. His many benefactions included paying for the restoration of the north porch at St Mary Redcliffe church. He sent his donations to the vicar under the pseudonym 'Nil Desperandum'— worry not.

Although he was a native of Birmingham Proctor quickly immersed himself in Bristol's civic affairs and was an alderman and High Sheriff. However, poor health prevented him from taking up the office of mayor.

When Proctor died flags were flown at half-mast on many of Bristol's public buildings.

Thomas Provis

(unknown)

It's hard to believe that Ashton Court Mansion, set in 840 acres of grass and woodland on the southern fringe of Bristol, was once at the centre of a most bizarre court case. It happened when a judge at the old Gloucestershire Assizes in 1852 was asked to determine the ownership of the estate after an astonishing claim by an impostor.

The house had been home to the Smyth family for more than 300 years when Thomas Provis arrived on the scene. Calling himself Sir Richard Smyth he claimed to be the long-lost heir to the family and its estate. He claimed that his father was Sir Hugh Smyth, a former owner of the property, who had died thirty years earlier.

Provis took his claim to court but the case turned sour for him when he was identified as a convicted horse thief by birth marks on his face and hands. The proceedings took another dramatic twist when a telegram arrived from a London jeweller stating that jewellery Provis claimed was a family heirloom had been engraved only a few months earlier.

Right until the end of the trial Provis still claimed to be a member of the Smyth family. However, the court did not believe his story and he was sentenced to twenty years transportation for perjury and forgery. Provis served only two years in jail before he died.

The Smyth family continued to live at Ashton Court until 1946 when the death of Mrs Esme Smyth brought to a close 400 years of ownership by the same family. The house and estate were later bought by Bristol City Council.

Sir Michael Redgrave

(1908—1985)

It is said that Sir Michael Redgrave was given his first name because his mother could see the tower of nearby St Michael's Church from the room in which she gave birth.

Michael Redgrave, whose parents were actors, was educated at Clifton College and went on to Cambridge where he wrote film reviews. His acting career began at the Liverpool Playhouse in 1934 after a spell as a schoolteacher. He arrived on the London stage two years later.

Sir Michael became one of Britain's greatest classical actors and also appeared in more than fifty films. One of his earliest screen roles was as the eccentric musicologist in Hitchcock's *The Lady Vanishes* in 1938.

He married the actress Rachel Kempson in 1935, a union which lasted fifty years until his death. The couple had three children, all of whom followed in their parents' acting footsteps.

In Bristol Michael Redgrave is commemorated by a plaque on his birthplace in Horfield Road, off St Michael's Hill, and the theatre at Clifton College is named after him.

Mary Robinson

(1758—1800)

Mary Robinson, who was nicknamed 'Perdita' after one of the Shakespear-ean roles for which she received acclaim, gave up a sparkling theatrical career to become mistress to the Prince of Wales, later George IV.

But when he rejected her she turned herself into a prolific novelist, pamphleteer, playwright and poet.

She was born Mary Darby in a house near Bristol Cathedral and attended the school run by The More sisters in nearby Park Street.

Mary's father abandoned the family for his mistress when she was still a child. By the age of fifteen she was living in London and wed to a law student called Robinson. The marriage was something of a disaster, lasting barely a year.

She then became one of London's most beautiful and celebrated actresses. Between 1776 and 1780 Mary played Perdita and other Shakespearean parts at Drury Lane.

Elisha Smith Robinson

(1817—1885)

Elisha Smith Robinson was the son of a paper-mill owner who founded what became one of the largest printing firms in the country. He arrived in Bristol in 1844 with just under £200 capital, about half of it borrowed from a friend. He initially set up his business in Baldwin Street supplying wrapping paper and paper bags to family-owned grocery and drapery shops. At first the bags were made by hand and later by machine.

An expanding order book led him to open a factory in Redcliffe Street in 1846 where he was joined two years later by his brother Alfred. For well over a century the firm traded as ES&A Robinson. The brothers, later joined by Alfred's two sons, introduced American techniques into their bag making and were pioneers in adapting lithographic printing for commercial and advertising use. By the end of the 18th century Robinsons were employing about 800 people.

Robinsons gradually expanded with factories across Bristol and in other parts of the country. Thanks to the foresight of Elisha the firm was turning out everything from cartons to disposable medical products. When the company merged with another stationary firm in 1966 the firm owned thirty other companies, employing around 10,000 people.

Elisha Robinson was also known as a benefactor helping to fund the building of the original Colston Hall in 1861.

Woodes Rogers
(1679—1732)

Captain Woodes Rogers was a privateer who led a swashbuckling life at sea during the early 18th century. He led a band of privateers who became wealthy by plundering treasure from Spanish galleons in the Caribbean and sacking towns.

In 1708 Woodes Rogers, who lived in Queen Square, set out on an expedition, financed by a powerful group of Bristol merchants, to take two ships, the *Duke* and the *Duchess*, around the world. Ostensibly the idea was to open up a trade route to the South Seas, but in effect this was a privateering voyage.

Rogers sailed to the South Sea and onto the East Indies before returning home around the Cape of Good Hope off South Africa. During his three years at sea, Rogers captured many Spanish ships and brought them to Bristol with their rich cargoes of booty. He also returned with the Scottish sailor Alexander Selkirk who had been marooned on the island of Juan Fernandez for four years.

Selkirk's experiences were told to Daniel Defoe, according to one legend by Selkirk himself, at the Llandoger Trow Inn, but whether the two men met or not makes no difference. Selkirk's adventures inspired Defoe to write his ever-popular story *Robinson Crusoe*.

Rogers himself wrote his own account of life at sea, *A Cruising Voyage Round The World*, which was published in 1719. A copy of the book, which had been lying in an attic, fetched £6,000 at auction in 2009.

King George I appointed Rogers as Governor of The Bahamas in 1717. He made it his policy to rid the islands of thousands of pirates with bribes, punitive action and pardoning.

Rogers died at his home in Queen Square where a plaque has been erected in his memory. It is inscribed:

Woodes Rogers 1679–1732
great seaman, navigator, colonial governor

Rt Rev Barry Rogerson

(1936—)

As Bishop of Bristol from 1985–2002 the Rt Reverend Barry Rogerson has gone down in ecclesiastical history for ordaining the first women priests into the Church of England.

He laid his hands on the heads of the first thirty-two women priests during an historic service in Bristol Cathedral in March 1994. It was the culmination of a most bitterly fought debate within the church since Henry VIII broke away from Rome.

Such was the importance of this service that it was beamed around the world in a live television broadcast with Bishop Rogerson laying his hands on the heads of the women ordinands.

Before studying theology at Leeds University and Wells Theological College, Barry Rogerson worked for a bank. His first church post was as a curate in South Shields. He came to Bristol from being Suffragan Bishop at Wolverhampton.

Now retired from full-time service he is an honorary assistant bishop in the diocese of Bath and Wells. He was made an Honorary Freeman of the City and County of Bristol in 2003, and now lives in retirement in North Somerset.

Peter Mark Roget

(1779—1869)

The name of Roget became famous for his *Thesaurus of English Words and Phrases*, a project on which he had worked for many years.

This son of a Swiss clergyman was a physician and scholar who had studied medicine. He was appointed physician to Manchester Infirmary in 1804 and for twenty-two years was Secretary of the Royal Society.

Roget had a special interest in tuberculosis and the effects of nitrous oxide which brought him to Dr Thomas Beddoes' Institution in Dowry Square, Hotwells. He wrote papers on this medical discovery, which had occured at Beddoes' institute.

But Roget is best known for his *Thesaurus*, a dictionary of synonyms, which was published in 1852 and has never been out of print.

Rajah Rammohun Roy

(1772—1833)

A beautifully restored ornate Grade II listed funeral monument in Arnos Vale cemetery is an important place of pilgrimage for people from all over the world. This is the resting place of Rajah Rammohun Roy, regarded as the founder of modern India.

He was a Brahmin, born in Bengal in 1772, who had extraordinary talents, and was fluent in many languages including English, Persian, Hebrew, Greek and Latin. He published newspapers and was a prolific writer on subjects ranging from grammar to geometry.

But Raja Rammohun Roy's great mission was to campaign for education for all and for other social reforms for his people, which he thought could flow from the establishment of a universal Indian religion. He also championed women's rights in India.

He visited England first in 1831 as the representative of the King of Delhi, who made him his ambassador and conferred upon him the title of Rajah. He visited many towns including Bristol, where he was interested in the work of social reformer Mary Carpenter.

Rajah Rammohun Roy was in Bristol again two years later but after ten days in the city was taken ill with meningitis from which he died. At first he was buried in the grounds of a friend's house at Stapleton Grove. But ten years later his remains were moved to their present resting place in Arnos Vale Cemetery.

Every September on the anniversary of his death, scores of pilgrims from India process to Raja Rammohun Roy's shrine to pay homage to their great compatriot. He is also commemorated by a statue made in India and shipped to Bristol for installation outside the central library on College Green.

James Sadler

(1753—1828)

Among the early aeronauts, as balloonists were then called, was James Sadler, the son of a confectioner, who made a flight from a field in Bristol in 1810.

Accompanied by William Clayfield, a chemist, he lifted off from Stokes Croft watched by a large crowd of spectators. But their balloon ran out of gas after a flight of around one hundred miles and came down with a splash when it ditched in the Bristol Channel off the North Devon coast.

Mr Sadler and Mr Clayfield were left floating around for an hour until they were rescued by the crew of a boat which was launched from Lynmouth. Undeterred by the experience James Sadler continued his ballooning activities.

Emma Saunders

(1841—1927)

Emma Saunders of Clifton who devoted most of her life to improving the lot of railway workers and their families earned the sobriquet the 'Railwaymens' Friend'.

Besides giving them flowers, shells and lavender bags, Miss Saunders also called upon the sick at their homes and became instrumental in setting up rest and recreation rooms for the men.

When the tunnel for the Bristol to Severn Beach line under the Downs was being excavated she started Sunday Bible classes for the men, and ran weekday meetings for their wives.

She was also a regular visitor to the train sheds at Temple Meads railway station handing out bunches of freshly-picked flowers from her garden in Sion Hill for the men to wear as button holes.

Every railway carter was given a copy of Anna Sewell's book *Black Beauty* in order to encourage them to treat their horses well.

Emma Saunders was so loved and respected that on her eightieth birthday, 5,000 railway workers contributed to a gift. She died on her eighty-sixth birthday, and four railwaymen shouldered her coffin through the streets to Christ Church for her funeral. Hundreds of men followed, all wearing their uniform and a daffodil in their buttonholes.

She is commemorated by a marble plaque outside the entrance to Temple Meads station on which she is depicted carrying a basket of flowers in one hand and a piece of paper in the other.

Alexander Selkirk

(1676—1721)

Alexander Selkirk's account of life as a shipwrecked sailor on a remote island in the South Pacific is the stuff of novels. Indeed his tale inspired Daniel Defoe to write his classic story *Robinson Crusoe*.

Selkirk, who was born in Fife, was rescued by Woodes Rogers, a privateer who was on a plundering voyage, from the island of Juan Fernandez, where he had been marooned for four years. Selkirk was a seaman who been put ashore after a quarrel with the captain of his ship. His only companions were goats and cats.

Selkirk was brought back to Bristol and popular legend has it that he met the writer Daniel Defoe in the Llandoger Trow on King Street, a public house near Rogers' home.

Ellen and Rolinda Sharples

(1769—1849 and 1794—1838)

On her death Ellen Sharples left Bristol a magnificent memorial. This is the building with the Italianate façade on Queen's Road in Clifton, the home of the Royal West of England Art Academy which was the city's first art gallery.

Four years before she died Mrs Sharples gave £2,000 towards the cost of building an academy, originally known as the Fine Arts Academy. In her will she bequeathed another £3,645 as well as one hundred pictures enabling the academy to open in 1858.

Born in Bath in 1769, she attended an art class and fell in love with her tutor, James Sharples, whom she married. They moved to America where the husband and wife painting team received commissions to paint portraits of prominent political figures including George Washington.

The Sharples family stayed in America until James died in 1811, when Ellen brought her children back to live in Clifton and set about bringing up her talented daughter Rolinda as a professional artist.

Rolinda Sharples was one of the first British women artists to tackle multi-figure compositions and is best known for her scenes of Bristol's social life in the 19th century. Her first major work was *The Cloak Room, Clifton Assembly Rooms*, which she completed in 1818. Other paintings depict the annual St James Fair and horse racing on Durdham Downs. Some of Rolinda's works can be seen in the Bristol Museum and Art Gallery.

Her life was cut short in 1838 by cancer when she was forty-four.

Frank Shipsides

(1908—2005)

It was Frank Shipsides' love of ships and the sea that brought him to Bristol. He arrived in the city from Nottingham in 1940 and stayed here for the rest of his life, becoming Bristol's favourite maritime artist.

He took up a job as an artist with Bennett Brothers, a printing firm, later moving to another local printer, Mardon Son & Hall, where he worked as senior artist for more than twenty years.

Frank Shipsides left the firm to freelance and decided to devote his time to serious painting in oils and watercolours. It meant that he was able to paint only what he wanted to paint. He quickly established a name for himself with his paintings of maritime Bristol and other local scenes. He recorded events like the return of the *SS Great Britain* and visits of the *Royal Yacht Britannia*. His first one-man exhibition in 1972 was an immediate sell out.

To honour the warship *HMS Bristol*, the city council commissioned him to paint seven large canvases of the ships that have borne the name of the city, commencing with a warship built by Oliver Cromwell.

Frank Shipsides was a noted book illustrator, an award-winning ship model maker and designer of theatre sets for the local stage. He was twice president of the group of artists known as Bristol Savages, and was given an honorary Master of Arts degree by Bristol University.

Among the many tributes paid to him at his death was one which described him as a 'national local treasure'.

Sarah Siddons

(1755—1831)

Local legend has it that the ghost of Sarah Siddons still haunts Bristol's Theatre Royal more than two hundred years after she trod the boards there.

Siddons, who became one of the greatest tragic actresses on the British stage, appeared at two Theatre Royals, at Bath and Bristol, in the years 1778—1782. She was a member of a joint company that was set up to perform in both cities. The actors shuttled by coach between the two theatres — sometimes in one day — for just £3 a week.

London theatre managements soon recognised her talents and Sarah Siddons became the 'queen of tragedy'.

She was the eldest child of a manager of a travelling theatre company and worked for her father as a child actress. She retired from the stage in 1812.

Viscount General Slim

(1891—1970)

His senior military colleagues knew him as 'the finest general World War II produced' and his troops called him 'Uncle Bill'. Such was the respect that William Joseph Slim commanded.

This son of an iron merchant was born in St Andrew's district of Bristol and lived in the city for the first twelve years of his life, until his family moved to Birmingham.

He joined the Army at the start of the First World War and served in Gallipoli and Mesopotamia. Much of his military career was spent in India and when the Second World War broke out he was sent out to head the Burma campaign, leading the famous 14th 'Forgotten Army' to victory over the Japanese. This was the largest unit ever in the British Army comprising men from twenty-eight nationalities.

After the war he was head of the Imperial General Staff, Britain's top military post, and was later Governor General of Australia.

When he was made a Viscount he took the name of Bishopston to commemorate the district of Bristol where his father was born. He was also awarded the DSO and the MC.

ACH Smith

(1935—)

Playwright Anthony Smith works under the name ACH Smith and is fondly regarded in Bristol for his much-loved community play *Up The Feeder, Down The Mouth*. This collage of music, oral history and theatre tells Bristol's story from the dockside and beyond.

It was first staged at the Theatre Royal and reworked four years later by Smith to include real life stories of dockers, mariners and their families. It was staged by the Bristol Old Vic on the city's Harbourside.

Smith's love of literature and journalism saw him editing the literary magazine *Delta* at Cambridge University. He joined the *Western Daily Press* in 1960, working alongside his lifelong friend, journalist turned dramatist Tom Stoppard. Both were working on the paper's arts page and were at the heart of a remarkable coterie of Bristol writers which also included Peter Nichols and Charles Wood.

His first literary efforts after leaving the *Western Daily Press* were novels, with the first, *The Crowd*, set in Bristol. Apart from plays he has also provided cricket reports for *The Times* and was involved in a long-running arts show for HTV.

The Smyth Family

The Smyth family originated from Lydney in the Forest of Dean. When they first arrived in Bristol the Smyths lived in a mansion in Small Street in the heart of the city. It was John Smyth, the merchant son of a cooper who bought Ashton Court mansion and its estate on the southern fringe of Bristol in 1545. It is doubtful if he ever lived at Long Ashton but when his elder son, Hugh, married in 1553 he gave him all his household goods in the house at Ashton Court and allowed Hugh and his wife to live there. For almost 400 years John Smyth's descendants lived at Ashton Court.

John Smyth became an alderman of Bristol and twice mayor of the city. As a merchant he was engaged in trade with Spain and France, exporting cloth, hides and Mendip lead in return for wine, iron and dyestuffs.

He founded a dynasty that became one of the most powerful in Bristol and North Somerset with the family becoming major landowners and benefactors in the city.

The Smyth's lived at Ashton Court until 1946 when the death of Mrs Esme Smyth brought to a close four centuries of ownership by the family. She was buried in Long Ashton churchyard. Thirteen years later Bristol Corporation, now Bristol City Council, bought the mansion and its grounds for £103,000 for use by people of the city for recreation and enjoyment. Since then large sums of money have been spent on restoring the mansion.

The house is now used for numerous events ranging from conferences to wedding receptions and the grounds are home to such annual events as the international balloon fiesta.

Robert Southey

(1774—1843)

Robert Southey, who was born in Wine Street where his father carried on a business as a draper, became one of the leading Romantic poets and Poet Laureate. He was christened in Christ Church just around the corner from his home.

Southey was educated at Oxford where he first met Coleridge. When he was twenty-one he married Elizabeth Fricker at St Mary Redcliffe Church. The groom had been lent the money for the wedding license and the ring by his publisher, John Cottle.

It was Cottle who paid £50 for Southey's first important work, *Joan of Arc*. He later edited a volume of Chatterton's poems which was also published by Cottle.

Although best known as a poet Southey also wrote a history of Brazil and of the Peninsula War as well as biographies of prominent people including John Wesley and Oliver Cromwell.

After living for a while at Westbury on Trym, Southey moved to Keswick in the Lake District where he spent the last forty years of his life. He was appointed Poet Laureate in 1813, a post he held until his death in 1843. Memorials to him can be found in Westminster Abbey and Bristol Cathedral.

William Spencer
(?—1493)

William Spencer was the instigator of one of the city's most spectacular and colourful ceremonies — the annual Rush Sunday civic service at St Mary Redcliffe church.

This one-time Mayor of Bristol was, it seems, desirous of getting more councillors to church, so in his will made provision for three sermons to be preached before the 'Mayor and Commonalty' on the Monday, Tuesday, and Wednesday after Whitsunday. The first services took place in 1494, the year after Spencer died, and the Rush Sunday ceremony has been held annually ever since. In his will Spencer left six shillings and eight pence for a sermon to be preached and three shillings for the Mayor, to entertain him to dinner. Down the centuries little seems to have changed to the Rush Sunday service save for reducing the sermons from three to one which was done at about the time of the Reformation.

The service takes its name from the rushes that are strewn over the floor of the church. The Lord Mayor, who arrives at the service in a horse drawn carriage with a mounted police escort, and the city councillors in their red robes, all walk over the rushes to their seats.

William Spencer, who also endowed an almshouse, is remembered in the naming of a block of flats in Redcliffe.

Rosemary Squires MBE

(1928—)

The world of show business is littered with stories of entertainers who come and go almost as quickly as the wind changes direction. But Bristol-born Rosemary Squires is still wowing the audiences after more than sixty years in front of the spotlights and has no plans to bring down the final curtain on her career just yet.

The theatrical spark in her life was lit when, as a five-year-old, she was taken to a pantomime at the Theatre Royal in King Street. During the interval the band accompanied a singer and Rosemary set her sights on a musical career.

In her teens she sang with local bands, later for soldiers on Salisbury Plain in Wiltshire, during the Second World War, followed by trips to Germany to entertain the British troops.

From an early appearance with Geraldo's band in the 1950s Rosemary was soon recording songs for major record labels both in this country and America. She has appeared with big bands and co-starred with everyone from Sammy Davis Jr to Danny Kaye and from Des O'Connor to Ken Dodd.

She has also recorded numerous television jingles, from her first for Fry's Turkish Delight, to what just might be the most famous and longest running one of all time, Fairy Liquid's 'hands that do dishes'.

Rosemary Squires now tours the country from Cumbria to Cornwall with three shows that she has devised with her husband. She was awarded the MBE in 2003 for services to music and charity.

She lives in Wiltshire, but is still a passionate lover of her home city and recalls childhood days at the family home on St Michael's Hill and going to the nearby Kingsdown Parade primary school.

Charlie Stephens

(1862—1920)

Charlie Stephens was a barber from West Street, Bedminster, who hankered for adventure, derring-do and danger. He often shaved his customers in a lion's cage in the backyard of the Red Cow public house watched by large numbers of spectators.

He also offered himself as a target for knife throwers at the Victorian music halls in Bristol, and even had an apple, balanced on his throat, sliced in two by a sword. Stephens also parachuted from a hot air balloon onto a railway track near his home just minutes before an express train was due.

But his stunt to top all stunts came in July 1920 when he shot himself over the Niagara Falls in a wooden barrel which had been specially reinforced with metal hoops. He loaded the bottom of the barrel with ballast in a vain attempt to keep it upright in the water. The barrel was topped with a lid which could be released from inside.

The barrel, with Charlie inside, was released into the water about two miles ahead of the Niagara Falls. For the crowds of spectators the last sight of the barrel and its occupant was halfway down the 160 foot drop. The next day parts of Charlie Stephens' arm were found in the water.

Back home at Bedminster his widow continued to run the hairdressing business.

Paul Stephenson OBE

(1941—)

Paul Stephenson made a stand on racism on Bristol's buses in 1963 which paved the way for Britain's first anti-racism laws.

Stephenson was a twenty-six year-old teacher and community officer when he led a victorious boycott against the then Bristol Omnibus Company over its policy not to employ any black or Asian drivers.

In the sixty-day boycott he was supported by thousands of Bristolians who refused to use the buses.

More than four decades later Paul Stephenson made history by becoming the first black person to have the Freedom of Bristol bestowed on him. This was in recognition of his 'extraordinary contribution' to the city through his public service and race relations work.

In 2009 he was awarded the OBE for his services to equal opportunities and to community relations in the city.

Rt Rev Dr Mervyn Stockwood

(1913 — 1995)

Known as the 'Red Bishop' because of his politics and outspoken views, Mervyn Stockwood started his church career in the impoverished parish of St Matthew, Moorfields, in East Bristol. He had been a Young Conservative but his experiences of deprivation amongst the parishioners led him to convert to socialism.

He was well known for his liberal views on divorce, abortion and homosexuality.

Mervyn Stockwood was brought to Bristol with his family when he was four years old. His father, a solicitor, had just been killed in the Somme in the First World War.

The young Stockwood attended All Saints Church, Clifton, where it seems the Anglo-Catholic liturgy helped him to set his sights on a career in the Church of England.

After serving as an assistant curate at St Matthew's for five years Mervyn Stockwood was made its vicar. Over the next fourteen years he became much loved for his pastoral care. He was also a Labour councillor on Bristol City Council for nine years.

From inner city Bristol he moved to Cambridge where he became vicar of Great St Mary, the university church. After only four years there he was offered the Bishopric of Southwark, a post he held for twenty years. In 1980 he retired to Bath where he died fifteen years later.

Mervyn Stockwood was one of the early advocates of women priests. In 1981 he went to America to ordain to the priesthood a woman he had previously made deacon in Southwark but who was barred from the priesthood in England.

Sir Tom Stoppard

(1937—)

The route from Bristol's newspapers to Fleet Street is well travelled. One young journalist that followed it in the 1960s went on to become one of Britain's best dramatists.

Playwright Tom Stoppard worked on both the *Western Daily Press* and *Bristol Evening Post* around that time. On the Press he was contributing to a newly introduced arts page. On moving to London he freelanced as a theatre critic and wrote radio plays, the first of which was broadcast in 1964.

His interest in the theatre started through his newspaper work which gave him the opportunity of meeting actors with the Bristol Old Vic Company including Peter O'Toole, who was with the company for four years.

Tom Stoppard made his name as a playwright with *Rosencrantz and Guildenstern Are Dead* which was premiered at the Edinburgh Festival in 1966 and transferred to the National Theatre, London.

Since then he has written a string of plays which have been produced on stages all over the world, including *Jumpers* and *Travesties* as well as television plays and film scripts. He has also dramatised Jerome K Jerome's *Three Men in a Boat* which had been brought out by the Bristol printer Arrowsmith a hundred years earlier.

Stoppard was born Thomas Straussier in Czechoslovakia and came to this country in 1946. In 1997 he was awarded a knighthood for services to the theatre.

Randolph Sutton
(1888—1960)

Randolph Sutton became known as Britain's premiere light comedian who was famous for his music hall songs with catchy titles such as *Where Do the Jam Jars Go?*, *Mrs Rush and Her Scrubbing Brush* and *On Mother Kelly's Doorstep*.

He began his singing career as a boy chorister at the local church. On leaving school he took work as a clerk but it seems that pen and paper pushing was never his forte. He soon left the job to join a seaside concert party as a singer-cum-comedian.

It wasn't long before Sutton made his first appearance on the London stage and eventually he set up his own road show which he took around the country. For many years he was a radio and stage superstar of his time. Audiences found it easy to sing along with his songs which had become antidotes to he hard times of the depression and the war.

He was commanded to appear at the Royal Variety Performance in 1948. As music hall went out of fashion, Sutton being the professional trouper that he was, turned to appearing in variety shows. His last appearance was at St Albans a few days before his death in 1960.

One of his friends, the late Poet Laureate John Betjeman, made a television programme based in Bristol as a tribute to Sutton. In 1963 Karl Denver, a Scottish singer, whose Western yodelling style had become popular, recorded one of Sutton's songs *My Canary Has Circles Under His Eyes* as another tribute.

A commemorative plaque can be found on Sutton's birthplace, a cottage in Anglesea Place, on the edge of Clifton Downs.

John Addington Symonds

(1840—1893)

John Addington Symonds was born in Berkeley Square and at fourteen was sent to Harrow School and then on to Balliol College, where he was awarded many prizes including a double first in Classics and a fellowship at Magdalen.

Symonds, the son of a much-respected physician who was one of the founders of the Bristol Royal Infirmary, became one of the major Englishmen of Letters towards the end of the 19th century. He had a prolific literary output, writing articles for leading periodicals, travel books, volumes of poetry and collections of essays as well as studies of Dante and the Greek poets. He was best known for his seven-volume *Renaissance in Italy*.

Though married, Symonds was an early advocate of homosexuality and openly referred to it in *The Meeting of David and Jonathan*, published in 1878. This was later followed up by one of the earliest essays defending homosexuality. He also published his own proposals for reforming anti-homosexuality law.

Symonds inherited his father's home, the Palladian mansion known as Clifton Hill House, though he, his wife Catherine North and their four daughters spent much time in Davos, Switzerland, the highest city in the world. As a sufferer of tuberculosis he found the climate there much kinder than in England. In Davos Symonds became friendly with another sufferer, the writer Robert Louis Stevenson. He was also a friend of the poet Edward Lear who wrote *The Owl and the Pussy Cat* for one of his daughters.

Clifton Hill House was acquired by Bristol University in 1909 for £55,000 and after adding extensions it became its first hall of student residence. It was an apt move as Symonds was instrumental in founding University College Bristol in 1876.

Dame Ellen Terry
(1848 —1928)

Before she trod the boards at the Theatre Royal when she was fifteen years old Ellen Terry had already appeared in pantomimes.

Ellen Terry, the daughter of theatrical parents, went on to become the leading Shakespearian actress in London sharing a memorable stage partnership with Henry Irving.

While in Bristol she had a liaison with William Godwin, an architect, theatre critic and costume designer. His home in Portland Square was a social centre for the artistic and literary set, but his affair with Ellen Terry was short lived, although she had two children with him.

After a lengthy career on the stage Ellen Terry went into theatrical management and made lecture tours of the country. She was honoured with a DBE in 1925.

Rev Urijah Thomas

(1839—1901)

A modest man with simple needs who spent much time helping others, the Reverend Urijah Thomas was one of the city's most respected and loved churchmen. At a time when there was no welfare state he threw himself into working with the poor.

The Rev Thomas was a Congregational minister who was the first incumbent of Redland Park Church on Whiteladies Road, serving it for forty years until his death.

On discovering the plight of so many people on what he called 'the verge of pauperism' he set up the Penny Dinner Society, which provided meals for them. So great was the need that in its first year in 1884 the society dished up some 52,000 dinners across the city.

Under Mr Thomas' guidance the society later set up a holiday camp for youngsters whose families could not afford for them to have an annual break away from home.

Initially, Barton Camp at Winscombe, was a very basic affair with wooden buildings serving as dormitories. Despite the somewhat primitive conditions Mr Thomas reasoned that if nothing else the youngsters would benefit from fresh country air and exercise by walking in the Mendip Hills.

Mr Thomas also helped found Redland High School and also set up the Ministers' Seaside home in North Devon, for clergy families in need of a break. The home ran until 1960.

When the Rev Thomas died Bristol witnessed the biggest funeral procession it had ever known. Streets were closed as huge crowds lined the route from Redland to Brislington as the cortege made its way to Arnos Vale cemetery.

As a memorial to Mr Thomas' contribution to society an ornate fountain surmounted by a clock tower and supported by marble columns was erected in his memory. It still stands in the midst of flowerbeds in the middle of Whiteladies Road near its junction with the Downs.

His Penny Dinner Society is still going strong although now known as the Bristol Children's Help Society. It may no longer serve up food but Barton Camp continues to give much-needed holidays to around 1,500 youngsters each year.

Brian Trubshaw

(1924—2001)

"It was wizard — a cool calm and collected operation", said Brian Trubshaw as he emerged from the cockpit of *Concorde 002*.

He had just fulfilled every schoolboy's dream of landing the British prototype of the supersonic aircraft after its maiden flight from its base at Filton, on the outskirts of Bristol, to RAF Fairford, Gloucestershire, in April 1969.

It was, he said, the highlight of his career which had started as an RAF pilot in the Second World War and later saw him as a member of the King's Flight. He piloted George VI and other members of the royal family.

Brian Trubshaw was a test pilot for thirty years and had been selected by the chairman of the British Aircraft Corporation to be Concorde's test pilot in the early days of the Anglo-French project. He became the corporation's Director of Test Flights.

His flying skills were recognised by the presentation of various industry awards. He was also made a Commander of the British Empire.

Brian Trubshaw became captivated by flight at the age of ten when he saw the Prince of Wales aircraft land on the beach at Pembrey, Carmarthenshire, not far from where his family then lived. This was a prelude to the Prince opening the Royal Welsh Agricultural Show.

Brian Trubshaw loved Concorde so much that he placed a weather vane depicting the aircraft on the roof of his home in the Cotswolds.

William Vick

(?—1754)

Wealthy wine merchant William Vick left £1,000 in 1754 to build a bridge across the River Avon at Clifton. He entrusted his endowment to the Bristol Society of Merchant Venturers with the instruction that it should be left to accumulate interest until the total fund reached £10,000.

Mr Vick stipulated that the money could then be used to build a stone bridge. He also left instructions in his will that the bridge be 'toll free for ever'.

By 1829 Mr Vick's fund had reached £8,700 and with other donations and a gift from the Merchant Venturers themselves £30,000 was eventually raised — enough to start work on the bridge.

Carol Vorderman

(1960—)

In the world of television game shows Carol Vorderman is something of a phenomenon. She appeared in every edition of *Countdown* since its inception until she left the show in 2008 — an unbroken twenty-six years.

Although the programme made Carol, who has a degree in engineering, a household name she has presented or created scores of other radio and television shows. Her credits range from a series on science to another explaining all about microchips. She has also written books and has made DVDs.

In 2009 Carol Vorderman was appointed by David Cameron, then leader of the Conservative Party, to lead a task force to examine how to make maths teaching in Britain's state schools as good as anywhere else in the world.

She moved to Bristol in 2007 having fallen in love with the city on her visits to her manager who has represented her for nearly twenty-five years. Carol's son and daughter are educated in the city while she runs her online teaching school for children from offices in Clifton.

Every year Carol Vorderman launches Run For The Future, a charity event which helps to raise funds for prostate cancer awareness, treatment and equipment. She also competes in the event, which is held on Durdham Downs every September.

William Watts

(18th century)

William Watts, a plumber, is said to have got the idea of making perfectly spherical lead shot from a dream in 1782. He used his wife's kitchen colander to carry out early tests, which proved successful!

Watts built the world's first purpose-built factory for making lead shot by adding a three-storey tower to his home on Redcliffe Hill. He also dug a shaft under the house through the caves underneath to achieve the required drop. The shot was made by pouring molten lead from a great height, through a perforated drum, into a pit filled with water.

Watts made a fortune from the business as lead shot was much in demand by the military for muskets and by farmers shooting pests.

However, he eventually sold the business along with his patent to Philip George, founder of the Bristol Brewery for £10,000. He spent the money on building the foundations of Windsor Terrace, Clifton. This absorbed all his funds and Watts, who was unable to proceed with the superstructure, became bankrupt. Other developers completed the fine terrace jutting out on the rock face from above Hotwells.

Although Watts' shot tower was officially designated by the government as a building of historical importance it was nevertheless demolished in 1968 to make way for road widening. His black tower had been a landmark for nearly two centuries.

Billy Wedlock

(1880—1965)

They called him the 'India Rubber Man' because of his ability to bounce so quickly into attack or defence. Some football fans still regard Billy Wedlock as Bristol City's greatest star although his last game was nearly a century ago. Football writers of the day described him as the most skilful centre half in the country.

Wedlock, affectionately known as 'Fatty' because of his stature, — he was just five feet four inches tall and weighing just under ten and half stone — was born in North Street, not far from City's ground at Ashton Gate. He played his first game for the club in 1900 when he was twenty years old.

For much of his career Wedlock skippered City and turned out for the club in 364 league games. He took the side to promotion in the 1905/06 season and was in City's FA Cup Final Side of 1909 which was defeated 1-0 by Manchester United. Wedlock was capped by England twenty-six times, and remains the most capped home international to have played for Bristol City.

After hanging up his boots for the final time Wedlock became landlord of the Star Inn opposite the club's main gate. He pulled pints there until a year before his death in 1965 at the age of eighty-four. In his honour the name of the pub, now demolished, was later changed to Wedlock's. A stand at the City ground is also named after him.

Fred Wedlock

(1942—2010)

The West Country vocalist and entertainer Fred Wedlock, grandson of Billy Wedlock, was paid for his first singing performance when he was just four years old! He received an old threepenny bit for entertaining customers in his father's bar.

Fred Wedlock was born and brought up in the York House, now the site of a car park opposite St Mary Redcliffe Church where he eventually became Head Choirboy.

After leaving Bristol Grammar School he worked variously in a youth employment office, department store and as a teacher. His growing popularity as a comic singer and raconteur prompted him to become a professional entertainer in the early 1970s.

Fred Wedlock shot to national fame at Christmas 1981 with a Top Ten hit called *The Oldest Swinger In Town* which was always a much-requested highlight of his stage act.

Television and radio shows followed, including a series with fellow West Countryman jazz man Acker Bilk, as well as a stint as a regional television presenter for Bargain Hunters.

He was constantly in demand by folk clubs, arts centres and colleges all over the country right up until his death in March 2010.

Wesley's Statue
Bristol. 31.

*Statue of John Wesley
outside the New Room,
Broadmead.*

John and Charles Wesley

(1703—1791 and 1707—1788)

Bristol has an important place in the history of Methodism, for it was here that its founder John Wesley built the first Methodist chapel in the world, known as the New Room.

Shortly after arriving in the city in 1739 Wesley bought a plot of land near the Horsefair on which his chapel, with its quaint double-decker pulpit, still stands. Wesley also built a stable for visiting preachers to keep their horses.

He delivered his first open air sermon to the people of Bristol in a brickyard in St Philips, which was packed with 3,000 people, on 1st April 1739. His last open-air meeting took place at Kingsdown in Bristol in 1790.

In the intervening years he had covered an estimated quarter of a million miles on horseback to preach 40,000 sermons. Many of his open-air meetings attracted large crowds of up to 14,000 people.

John's brother Charles — they were two of nineteen children in the family —lived for a while in Charles Street, Stokes Croft, not far from the New Room. It was here that Charles wrote some of his 6,500 hymns. Many of them, including *Love Divine* and the rousing Christmas carol *Hark the Herald Angels Sing,* are still popular today.

William West

(1801—1861)

Artist and amateur astronomer William West was responsible for one of the city's most unusual buildings, the observatory on Clifton Down, which he built on the site of an old windmill. West had rented the ruins of the windmill which had been virtually destroyed by fire from the Society of Merchant Venturers.

Apart from a home for himself West built a tower which he fitted out with telescopes, a camera obscura and various astronomical instruments.

The camera obscura at the top of the tower still reflects a 360-degree panoramic view of Clifton, taking in the Avon Gorge and the Suspension Bridge, onto a white five-foot diameter bowl shaped viewing table in a darkened room below.

The entrepreneurial West also spent two years excavating a passage underneath the observatory to create a link to a cave below. It took him two years to blast through the 200-foot-long passage which was opened in 1837. A viewing platform, which is still a popular attraction, was installed at the end of the tunnel.

William West died in 1861 but his relatives continued to live at the observatory until 1943.

Sir George White

(1854—1916)

George White not only left his mark on his native Bristol but also across the United Kingdom as a businessmen, industrialist and promoter of tramway systems. He also founded the British and Colonial Aeroplane Company which was responsible for many developments in civil and military aviation.

George White came from a humble background. His father was a decorator while his mother was a lady's maid. When he left school at fourteen, he joined Stanley and Wasbrough, a local firm of commercial lawyers, as a junior clerk. There he was put in charge of the Law Society Library.

After just two years with the company, George White took charge of the bankruptcy side of the business. A further two years on he formed the syndicate which became the Bristol Tramway and Carriage Company, of which he later became secretary, managing director and chairman.

Using his financial skill George White set up his own stockbroking business. The local press revelled in his financial deals, the type of which was normally carried out in the City of London.

He also opened the first electric tramway service in Bristol — the first in Great Britain — in 1895, and became involved in similar systems across the country.

In 1910 George White founded the British and Colonial Aeroplane Company (later the Bristol Aeroplane Company) at Filton which has now become one of the largest aerospace complexes in Europe. Amongst White's first planes were the *Bristol Boxkite* and the *Bristol Fighter*.

In later life he became a philanthropist and was largely responsible for raising enough funds to build a major extension to the Bristol Royal Infirmary.

George White was made a baronet in 1904. He died suddenly in 1916 and was buried in St Mary's Church, Stoke Bishop.

But for all that he did for Bristol, Sir George is now hardly recognised in the city apart from a small plaque on his birthplace in St Michael's Buildings, Kingsdown, and a street named after him in the 2008 Cabot Circus shopping and leisure complex.

Reverend Dr Thomas White

(1550—1624)

Almost four hundred years after his death the Reverend Dr Thomas White is still remembered at the almshouse he founded with a special feast on the anniversary of his birthday.

This son of a clothier was born in Temple parish and went to Oxford University, afterwards training for a career in the church. For nearly half a century he was Rector of St Dunstan's-in-the-West in London's Fleet Street.

The Reverend White also held a number of other prestigious ecclesiastical posts, including that of a Prebendary at St Paul's Cathedral. He was also a Canon of Christ Church, Oxford, and of St George's Chapel, Windsor.

He returned to Bristol in 1613 to set up Temple Hospital (almshouse) in Temple Street, not far from his birthplace. This provided accommodation for ten people — eight men and two widows — whom Thomas White selected and called 'the brothers and sisters'.

On his death at the age of seventy-four he left instructions in his will for a feast to be held at the Almshouse every December 21 — the Feast Day of the Apostle Thomas and the date of his own birthday. He bequeathed forty shillings for the meal and stipulated that special pewter plate be used for the occasion. His instructions were that baron of beef and apple pie should be on the menu along with a quince to add flavouring.

This special meal still takes place, although not on such a grand scale, with parts of Dr White's will being read to the almshouse residents, its trustees and the Lord Mayor of Bristol.

Dr White also left funds for repairing some of Bristol's roads and provided for outfits for young women going into domestic service.

His almshouse has been rebuilt several times and now stands in Prewett Street in the shadow of St Mary Redcliffe church spire.

John Whitson

(c1557—1629)

John Whitson was an orphan born in Clearwell in the Forest of Dean who came to Bristol in his early teenage years with nothing, but eventually became one of the city's most colourful and influential self-made men.

He was Member of Parliament for Bristol four times and was twice Mayor of the city, and was also a Master of the Society of Merchant Venturers.

Whitson started work as an apprentice to a wine cooper and ship owner. On his employer's death he married the widow and took over the business. This was the first of three marriages to three widows.

As a successful merchant he had shares in a ship that made an expedition from Bristol to the New World in 1603. The captain reached a harbour which he named after Whitson, but which later became known as Plymouth.

Whitson nearly lost his life while sitting in court as a magistrate trying to settle a long-standing dispute between two men. The historian John Latimer records in his Annals of Bristol that:

> *a shocking attempt to murder Alderman Whitson took place... one of the men pulled out a knife, rushed upon Alderman Whitson and dealt him a violent stab in the face, penetrating through the cheek and nose into the mouth.*

He recovered from the wound and bequeathed a legacy to St Nicholas Church for an annual sermon to commemorate his escape. He died two years later after falling from his horse.

Whitson also left a grant of £90 a year to provide a 'fit convenient dwelling house' for forty girls whose parents were 'deceased and decayed'. He gave instructions that they were to be taught English and should be 'apparelled in red cloth', hence the school's name of Red Maids.

Every November staff and students celebrate Whitson's Day with a special ceremony in the crypt of St Nicholas Church when they lay a wreath on his tomb. Afterwards the girls, many of them wearing red, bring a splash of colour to the city as they process from the church to Bristol Cathedral for a service.

Whitson's school began its life at College Green but now stands in pleasant grounds at Westbury-on-Trym and is the oldest girls' school in the country.

The Wills Family

The Wills tobacco family have long been at the forefront of the city's life. It all started when Henry Overton Wills, the son of a clockmaker from Salisbury arrived in Bristol in 1786 and went into partnership with Samuel Watkins making pipe tobacco in Castle Street. Five years later the firm moved to Redcliffe Street and when Henry Wills died, his sons WD and HO Wills took over the business.

As cigarettes became popular the firm outgrew its premises and the brothers built factories in Bedminster and Ashton to meet the demand for their various brands. Factories were built in Belfast, Glasgow and Newcastle, too.

The elder son William met an unfortunate death when he was knocked down by a horse bus in London in 1865. About 2,000 people turned up for his funeral at Arnos Vale.

In its heyday the firm was making 350 million cigarettes a week providing work for thousands of families. It was often said that a job with Wills was a job for life. However, the decline in smoking helped to bring about the end of cigarette making in Bristol towards the end of the 20th century.

Bristol has many memorials to the generosity of the Wills family. It was HO Wills (the second) who endowed the University of Bristol in 1909 with a gift of £100,000. He was appointed its first Chancellor.

The university's 215-foot neo-Gothic university tower standing sentinel-like at the top of Park Street, and called the Wills Memorial Building, was built in his memory. It was the idea of brothers Sir George and Mr Henry Herbert Wills who wanted to mark the deeds of their father.

Over the last hundred years at least thirteen members of the family have died millionaires, together leaving more than £45 million. They were involved with many institutions in the city, among them the City Art Gallery and Museum, Victoria Rooms and homeopathic hospital. They also laid the foundation stones of some thirty congregational churches.

Many members of the family have held leading roles in the running of the Society of Merchant Venturers. In civic life they provided a number of sheriffs for Bristol. The late Sir John Wills was the first, and only, Lord Lieutenant of the County of Avon which was formed in 1974 embracing Bristol, parts of South Gloucestershire and North Somerset. The new county was abolished two decades later in another round of local government boundary changes.

William Wyrcester (or Worcester)

(1415—c1485)

Long before the day of Ordnance Survey maps Bristol had its own topographer. He was William Wyrcester, the son of a local tradesman, who measured buildings and streets simply by pacing them.

His detailed survey of Bristol in 1480 which included roads, quays and churches was, apparently, so accurate that it helped craftsmen to restore important buildings like St Mary Redcliffe church.

He travelled all over England recording the measurements of towns, their public buildings and the distances between them.

At one time Wyrcester was a retainer of Sir John Falstaff in Norfolk, becoming his executor, but he returned to Bristol, settling in St James Back. He is commemorated in a stained glass window in St Mary Redcliffe.

Ann Yearsley

(1756—1806)

Not everyone who delivers the daily pint of milk has their portrait in the National Portrait Gallery in London. But that happened to Bristol milk lady Ann Yearsley. Remarkably, there's not just one portrait of her in the gallery's archive collection but four.

Ann delivered milk to families in the large houses around Clifton but also had a talent for writing poetry, historical plays and novels and became known as 'Lactilla' or 'the Bristol milk woman'.

Fortune came her way after she showed some of her verses to a cook to whom she delivered milk. The cook, in turn, showed the poetry to her mistress who happened to be Hannah More, philanthropist, patron of the arts and a playwright herself.

Miss More set about getting Ann Yearsley's poems published and eventually found a thousand subscribers for a leather volume entitled *Poems on Several Occasions*. It was published to much acclaim bringing in some £600.

But the financial returns from Ann Yearsley's work were the cause of a split in her friendship with Hannah More, who had suggested the money should be put into a trust fund. The poet thought her benefactor was trying to keep it and insisted on taking it, rapidly losing the lot.

In 1791 Ann Yearsley wrote an historical tragedy in verse, *Earl Goodwin*, which was performed at Bath and Bristol, and later published an historical novel, *The Royal Captives*.

She also set up a circulating library at The Colonnade, Hotwells. Despite her brief period of fame Ann Yearsley died in obscurity at Melksham, Wiltshire. She was buried in Clifton churchyard.

EH Young
(1880—1949)

Emily Hilda Young could often be seen strolling the streets of Clifton and kicking up the leaves as she wandered across the Downs seeking inspiration for her books. Writing under the name EH Young she published eleven novels, several of which were adapted for broadcast as radio plays, short stories and children's literature.

Some of her novels were set in Upper Radstowe, a name that Emily Young invented for Clifton. Its streets took on new guises too, with The Mall, for example, becoming The Barton. Canynge Square was renamed Chatterton Square.

Emily Young arrived in Bristol from Northumberland in 1902 and married a local solicitor, Arthur Daniell. The couple lived in a top floor flat in elegant Saville Place, off Regent Street.

After her husband died in a battle at Ypres in 1917 during the First World War, Emily Young moved to London. She lived there in a *ménage a trois* with Ralph Henderson, headmaster of Alleyne's School, Dulwich, as her lover. His wife was living in the same house.

When he retired Ralph Henderson moved with Emily to Bradford-on-Avon where she died.

Afterword

Every city has its own peculiar atmosphere which is largely due to the people who live there. Bristol has plenty to be proud of when it comes to famous people. Some were born in the city and others who were drawn to it by its colourful heritage, adventurous spirit and vibrant atmosphere of culture and enterprise.

Whether they were poets, painters, scientists, explorers or even eccentrics they left their mark on this ancient city adding another chapter to its deep-rooted history. They have also helped to keep Bristol at the forefront of advances in such fields as aeronautical engineering, medicine, commerce, the arts and media technology.

Whilst many of these remarkable people and their activities have become the stuff of history books, others are unsung sons and daughters of Bristol. It was to help keep their names alive that this book was written.